Getting Closer
Sex, Love and Common Sense

OPTIMA

Getting Closer

Sex, Love and Common Sense

John Button

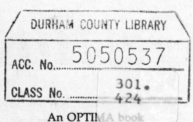

An OPTIMA book

© John Button 1992

First published in 1992 by Optima,
a division of Little, Brown and Company (UK) Ltd

A catalogue record for this book is available from the British Library

ISBN 0 356 20566 5

Little, Brown and Company (UK) Ltd
165 Great Dover Street
London SE1 4YA

Designed and typeset by the author
using Ventura Publisher

Printed and bound in Great Britain by
Cox & Wyman Ltd
Reading, Berkshire

Contents

Introduction

'So what's this one about?' ask my friends as they learn that I'm working on a new book. 'Is it another green book? I would have thought there were quite enough of those by now.'

'Not exactly,' I say, wondering how to frame my answer to match what they know of the therapeutic work I do alongside my environmental activism. If they don't know much about the workshops I run on relationships, communication and sexuality, I usually say, 'Well, it's about communicating better in close relationships.' If they know better this side of my work, I elaborate. 'It's about sex and gender,' I say, 'and AIDS, and love, and friendship, and co-operation, and fulfilment. It's about alternatives to oppressive and limiting ideas about the way people relate to each other.'

'Oh yes,' most of them say, with a discernible degree of self-interest. 'Have you discovered anything new?'

'Well, yes and no,' I say. 'Almost everything I say has been said before by someone, but I've never seen it all brought together. And I've tried to make it all as accessible as possible by not using difficult language.'

'Sounds interesting,' they say. 'Can I read it?'

'When I've finished writing it,' I say.

As I write and read and think and talk with people about friendship and sexuality, important ideas keep clicking into place. Especially as I read the growing amount of therapeutic and self-help literature, or listen to people's experiences as they try to sort these issues out for themselves, I realise that many people are reaching the same sort of conclusions. It isn't really very surprising when we are all attempting to get back to commonsense principles concerning human behaviour. This realisation has helped me to sort out the basic assumptions I have made in this book. The three assumptions I've made are:

❀ That everybody is limited by the roles imposed upon them, and that it is in everybody's interests to explore ways of overcoming these limitations.

❀ That beliefs about sex-related characteristics need to be very carefully examined. Assumed differences between men and women should automatically be suspect, since they arise from a prevailing belief system that expects to find such differences, and that nearly always operates to the disadvantage of women. Put another way, I assume that women and men have identical potential until it is unquestionably proven otherwise.

❀ That everybody (with the possible exception of new-born babies) has been hurt and damaged by experiences related to sexuality and sexual differentiation, and would benefit greatly from looking at these experiences and their results.

Some of my questioning friends are feminist women, who understand very clearly that most expectations about the way that people relate have been formulated by men. Like so much else in our male-oriented society, men have organised things to their own advantage under the disguise of democratic concern and fatherly benevolence. These friends point out, not that I hadn't noticed, that I am a man, brought up as one of a privileged class with no direct experience of the oppression felt by women. My world view is therefore very suspect.

I accept this justified wariness, but I've been living with the contradiction for a long time now. What I do know is that between my experience of being with people, especially people who are experimenting with alternative lifestyles, and my talking with and reading the books of writers who have been influenced by the women's movement, I have begun to see that we all have a lot of ideas in common. And the more I try to live my life according to the general beliefs I have set out as the assumptions of this book, the more I enjoy myself, and the more I can help others and myself to be straightforward, emotionally honest, and physically and mentally fulfilled in our relationships. It's not always easy; the conditioning goes very deep and it often feels very frightening to do things in completely new ways. But then, as Gertrude Stein once said, 'Considering how dangerous everything is, nothing is really very frightening.'

The octogenarian feminist Dora Russell, talking to Dale Spender for her book *There's Always Been a Women's Movement This Century*, asks 'Must we forever go on fighting, trying to rid ourselves of male power and its abominable consequences? Can't men see that they are destroying themselves, us, the planet, the species? Is there no way for us to live in co-operation and harmony with each other, with our fellow human beings, our fellow creatures?'

As I fervently believe that we must continue to work for a healthier and more just world in the hope and expectation of positive change, so I have to believe that the answer is that there must be a way forward. And I confess, somewhat against an inner voice that tells me not to be so dogmatic, that I have to believe that my conclusions about friendship and sexuality are at least roughly correct, otherwise I don't see much of a future for love and co-operation between people.

1

Friends in a Sea of Confusion

Intimate friendship is having a hard time at present. You might say that's always the nature of close relationships, but in these paradoxical days of freedom and reactionary backlash, openness and fear, AIDS and 'safer sex', the promise of truly satisfying intimacy can often seem more of an unattainable fantasy than ever before.

The world we live in is changing very quickly and, despite resistance to change, one of the things that is changing most rapidly is the way that human beings relate to one another. For better or for worse, many of the 'rules of engagement' between people as they get close to each other have become little more than quaint historical curios. New rules, rapidly changing and better learnt by some than by others, now apply. Meanwhile, though our behaviour may have changed, many of our deep-seated attitudes and prejudices survive from those more staid and predictable times when people simply 'knew their place'.

What we are left with is an almost impenetrable morass of old assumptions and new confusions. We know that there has to be something beyond stereotyped and oppressive sex-role behaviour, but those who enjoy and benefit from the games are unwilling to allow the rules to be changed. We know that we need support, acknowledgement, fulfilment, warmth, closeness. But we also know that it's precisely at the times when we express these needs openly that we are most likely to get hurt. Once bitten, twice shy – and by the time we've been bitten three or four times we have probably convinced ourselves that the vulnerability of intimacy simply isn't worth the pain.

Then there are all those feelings that arise when we get really close to someone else: the elation and joy, the fear and pain, the frustration and anger. One minute we're afraid they'll go away and leave us for ever, the next we're afraid that they'll never stop clinging to us. Is there any real hope for pain-free love and intimacy?

Then, just as we were beginning to sort out some of these relationship conundrums, thinking that there might be a way of organising our lives so that we could meet just a few of our fundamental needs for warmth and openness, along came AIDS. For several years it was a vague threat, lurking just below the horizon of everyday reality. By the late 1980s, however, it had become all too real, with black gravestones clanging on our television screens and the gay community suffering from ever more vicious discrimination.

AIDS is still a rare disease and, contrary to popular mythology, does not always result in a swift and inevitable death. Yet partly because it links our culture's four main taboo subjects – sex, death, drugs and homosexuality – and partly because it refuses to succumb to mainstream medicine, the disease has caught the popular imagination in a unique way.

The first British AIDS case was diagnosed in 1981; nine years later the most recent figures show 3,798 cases, of whom 2,040 have died. The number of people in this country known to be HIV positive is now 14,723. AIDS is still predominantly a homosexual phenomenon (in Britain accounting for 80 per cent of the figures). But the rate of increase of homosexual cases is slowing, while the opposite is true for heterosexuals. 'Cases of AIDS in this group are increasing faster than in any other,' comments Sir Donald Acheson, the government's Chief Medical Officer. 'During 1990-91 the number of cases of AIDS acquired by heterosexual intercourse has risen by 95 per cent, from 123 to 240, and cases in women by 72 per cent, from 104 to 179. It is vitally important that heterosexual people adopt safer behaviour patterns.'

This word 'safe' has, within a few short years, become the keyword of relationship advice and sex education. In the early 1980s the books about relationships exhorted us to express ourselves, communicate clearly, discover what fulfils us. These days, and without having thought too much about the ramifications and implications, everyone is telling us to ensure that we keep safety uppermost in our minds. A book written by Celia Haddon and Thomson Prentice and endorsed by the British Medical Association Foundation for AIDS is called *Stronger Love, Safer Sex*. A government AIDS press campaign tells us to 'Enjoy life; play safe'. Almost every one of the recent torrent of self-help relationship books exhorts us to keep things safe. 'There is only one way to protect against the fatal AIDS,' says Sandra Kahn in *The Ex-Wife Syndrome*: 'Always make sure the man uses a condom during sexual intercourse'.

If only it was as simple as that to stay safe. It's too easy to replace one set of moral rules with another, however well-meaning. But setting out – or even keeping to – inflexible moral codes will never reflect accurately the complexity of human needs, aspirations, hopes and fears. Thus it comes as no surprise to discover that people simply aren't doing what they are being advised to do.

A 1990 study of sixty Norfolk teenagers by Jo Frankham and Ian Stronach, entitled *Making a Drama out of a Crisis*, concluded that many are suffering from 'AIDS Invulnerability Syndrome'. They know the HIV and AIDS messages but reject 'safer sex', worry about pregnancy rather than disease, and have a very low opinion of sex education.

'What the media are trying to do is make AIDS sound like a big problem,' says seventeen-year-old John. 'They shove some figures down your throat, and my personal feeling is they've made it worse than it really is to stop you having sex.' Gill, aged fifteen, agrees. 'It's like smoking,' she says. 'You look at a cigarette and don't connect it with lung cancer and it's almost the same – I don't connect sex with disease.'

While many of the teenagers in the study dismissed the AIDS threat completely, others preferred to acknowledge that there is a problem – but not where they live. 'People in London or Edinburgh might be HIV positive, but everybody knows everybody round here. You can't get away with anything,' says fourteen-year-old Wendy. 'People would know if anyone in their neighbourhood had got it.'

Most of the teenagers in the study ignore all the 'safe sex' advice, relying instead on the post-sixties traditional contraceptive, the pill. As seventeen-year-old Gary says, 'If I knew the girl, if I'd been friendly with her or knew her for a long time, I'd ask her if she was on the pill or something. In that case, if I knew her, I'd probably have sex without using a condom.'

Suzie Hayman, the author of a frank Brook Advisory Centre booklet called *Say Yes, Say No, Say Maybe?*, believes that people are just plain confused. Bombarded with ill thought out advice and warnings, she says, there is every reason to go for a head-in-the-sand response. 'People are getting very confused about safe sex. I talked to a couple last week who thought that mutual masturbation meant masturbating in front of each other. How could they know differently if they'd never come across the term before?'

Much of the problem about 'safe behaviour' arises because 'not being safe' covers such a wide spectrum, from downright foolhardiness to refusing to engage in anything unless it is completely familiar and thoroughly tested. When it comes down to it, most of what the experts are warning us against is foolhardiness. But the fine distinctions between different sorts of risk-taking are simply not being understood. When people are confused about the relative risks involved in different kinds of behaviour, it is hardly surprising that the whole subject of intimacy becomes wrapped in a fine mist of insecurity.

This is nothing new. Since every aspect of intimate behaviour has for years been surrounded by fear and secrecy, it is almost by its nature unsafe. 'Safe sex' is, to put it bluntly, a contradiction in terms – for most teachers and advisers as well as for pupils and clients. However, whilst AIDS has succeeded in frightening us profoundly, it has at least brought our most deep-seated fears about sexuality and intimacy into the full light of day. More importantly, it has encouraged us to think very clearly about what we really want when we think we need sex.

Marek Kohn makes this point very clearly in the May 1987 issue of *The Face* magazine, when she writes:

> AIDS changes what is possible in sex, but that does not mean sex is simply going to get worse. People may decide that, instead of business as usual plus condom, they may get more physical and emotional pleasure by giving more time and care to their relationships. Restrictions on sexual freedom could lead to a world of lifeless partnerships held together by fear and a resurgent conservatism, in which purity and virgins are at a premium. They could also encourage people to value friendship more highly, and

to reconsider the code of sexual precedence which holds that only heterosexual intercourse counts, and that anything else is either juvenile or perverse. Wouldn't it be better to try and create a new world out of the disaster, rather than letting the old one take over?

There are few people who would deny the importance of close and intimate friendship. Friendship is about mutual sharing, trust, honesty and support. Friendship is about being yourself in relation to someone else, about being with them and learning to love them, about understanding and sympathy. We are closer to some friends than to others: there are the few with whom we share our secrets, our hopes and our fears; and then there are some with whom we share our bodies and our sexuality.

Here, if we are not careful, the old romantic tale takes over, the plot we have so carefully learned. We have been told that the highest and most important form of relating goes beyond mere friendship, where we share not only our observations and thoughts, our feelings and our bodies, but also that most intimate of things, sex. Through sex, the story continues, we can transcend the barriers that keep us apart, and come to a deeper understanding of what binds people together. With a lover it is possible to feel a unity with nature, a togetherness that goes beyond individuality, a oneness that reaches to the very heart of human nature.

Well, something like this can sometimes be true. But our sexual behaviour often tells us more about social conditioning than it does about human nature. For example, as Angela Carter so cleverly points out in *The Sadean Woman*, the primal nakedness of lovers – that innocence that would be spoilt by talking about it too much – can only be enjoyed in more northerly climes by the proud possessors of central heating. The poorer of us enjoy our intimacy under bedclothes, usually in the dark. Sexual sophistication, fondly believed to be the expression of natural passion, is frequently a by-product of education, advertising and money. In human relationships we can afford to take very little for granted.

Years of increasing confusion, of not knowing which story to believe, have resulted in an ever-growing lack of self-confidence. As we have lost confidence in ourselves, we have also lost the ability to become equal partners in relationship with others. Too often we are neither able nor prepared to look at the potential within ourselves for changing our lives, and so have reached the stage where we have difficulty in appreciating what friendship actually is.

Relating to and working with other people provides much of the interest and variety in life. But not all. As we walk alone along a deserted beach or under the stars on a clear wintry night, or curl up by the fire with a good book, we occasionally realise that we can be satisfied with our own company, and that our lives are not completely dependent on our interaction with others.

For many people this doesn't happen very often, and their lives are so tied up with other people that moments of complete self-fulfilment are rare. Clinging to the people around them, the small part of their lives spent alone is often used to worry about whether they feel lonely, an inevitable reaction to a society that ridicules the recluse and finds so many reasons to pity anybody who doesn't have a 'proper' relationship.

Even people who do know what rewards solitary self-fulfilment can bring must also be aware that the walk along the beach or the inward moment of self-reflection can all too easily be shattered, or at least infiltrated, by the remembered words and actions of other people.

Despite a renewed interest in meditation and other techniques of learning to be complete within ourselves, there is a deep lack of the solitary in Western society. Many people's worst fear is to be alone, completely alone, for more than an hour or two. To be seen as 'a loner' suggests that something is wrong, that a person doesn't have the necessary social skills.

The hazy borderlands between solitude and loneliness have been commercialised with a vengeance in recent years. Twenty years ago the conventional transition in late teens or early twenties was from family home to lifelong marriage. With more people leaving home earlier and the increasing breakdown of marriage, a new singles industry has flourished, fuelled by the fervent desire of younger and younger teenagers not to be left out of this exciting world of clubs, bars and discos, singles holidays and computer dating. The professed aim of the singles industry is to bring together potentially lonely people, and if there is money in it, so much the better. There is a substantial financial reward to be gleaned from persuading people that they are lonely.

The message that many single people receive is that singleness is a problem, if not a social disease. This is especially true for women, since it is popularly believed that women cannot really exist in their own right, and that the common aim of all single women is to get married. Spinsterhood has borne a stigma that bachelorhood has escaped, and the same male-dominated belief system has also decreed that men remain attractive most of their lives while women deteriorate and wither away, especially if they don't have a man to remain attractive for. In so many ways we are taught to fear solitude and to judge ourselves by our attachment to someone else. No wonder being single is shunned. The question on the lips of so many lonely people is 'Why can't *I* find someone?'

Changes in the pattern of friendship have helped to cultivate the phenomenon of loneliness in our society. When most people were born, grew up and died in the same community, the making of friends was a much more straightforward process than now. The choice was much more limited, the horizon narrower, but there was much less room for people to be ignored unless they chose to be.

Increased mobility – the ability to move in search of education, work and leisure – has drastically changed the nature of friendship. Most people no longer live in the same place for most of their lives, getting to know the people around them from years of regular association. Where people live close to each other only for short periods, it becomes much more important to make connections quickly and, apart perhaps from immediate neighbours, people tend to meet through planned groups and organisations rather than through chance encounters. The office party, the political action group, the parent-teachers association and the church group take over from the high street huddle. Even where the pub or the park are available as potential meeting places, arrangements to meet are most often made beforehand, and the hope of making a new friend in such circumstances is generally a forlorn one.

Social mobility has increased too, and people have more opportunity than ever before to mix with people from different social, economic and racial backgrounds. The potential for mutual understanding, and the opportunities to cross the barriers of class, interest, nationality and age have never been greater. Yet the often unspoken language of potential friendship, difficult enough to interpret when the participants have the same background, often becomes increasingly open to misinterpretation between people with different cultural and social assumptions.

A third radical change in the pattern of friendship is the change in the structure of the family. The small family, with two generations living in their own separate accommodation for a mere sixteen or seventeen years before the children move on, has become standard throughout most of the Western world. Children may hardly know their grandparents or cousins, their friendships often being confined to a group of children of their own age and background.

While the extended family has become relatively unimportant, our immediate family are the people to whom the majority of us relate the most closely. We are almost bound to relate to them – parents, children, sisters and brothers. In the way we use the phrase 'family and friends' there is the assumption that our family relationships are quite different from our other friendships. Many theorists on love have made the distinction between the love between parents and children, the love between sisters and brothers, and the love between sexual lovers.

It's certainly true that most of us spend more time with the people in our family than with anybody else, and it's also true that we can't choose our biological family. Sometimes, though we don't often like to admit it, we feel trapped in our family, stuck with people whose company we might not always choose if they weren't related to us. So our family is different from our friends.

Then there are our partners, typically somebody of the other sex, with whom we share space, and often our bed and some of the care of our children. Our partners, too, stand apart from our friends, and again the language we use brings this home. Most of us will have reached a point in a relationship when we were asked with a wink, 'Are you still just good friends then?' The hoped-for response is, of course, 'No, we're going out together now', or (and the two answers don't seem to contradict each other) 'No, we're living together now.' So our partners too are something different, in a category apart from our friends.

Which leaves our friends, our real friends, the people we are 'just' friendly with, as opposed to being related to or being attached to.

We expect to be intimate with our partner and physically close to our family. Friends are different, especially other-sex friends. The conventionally pre-ordained and often unspoken link between intimacy and involvement makes it very difficult to convey a wish or an intention only to be physically close and not sexually intimate, or sexually intimate and not totally involved. Where this is linked with dubious assumptions about the nature of sexuality and sex roles, a pattern of total confusion in relationship emerges.

Then there is the question of possession. Phrases like 'my wife', 'my children' and 'my boyfriend' often set up invisible territorial limits around people in pairs and groups, and it becomes very difficult to reconcile the expected behaviour of 'my' people with the acceptance that they too are human and need to define themselves for themselves. The working through of this apparent paradox is the basis for an understanding of possessive and non-possessive love, a subject that will arise again in Chapter 7.

Another problem is the creation of neat categories of relationship, and the abandon with which we try to bang the square pegs of reality into the round holes of our categories. The concept of friend is a particularly difficult one to define and, rather than striving to create ill-defined categories for friendship, I think that it's more rewarding to look for the common features of all relationships. We have the possibility of reinstating the concept of friendship as a fairly neutral term to cover the multitude of relationship words we use at present, words that are often sinking under the combined weight of *double entendre* and unnecessary role-associations.

Next comes the pervasive connection in our culture

between friendship and romance. Far from being the reasonably well-defined phenomenon of medieval chivalric etiquette it once was, romance is now a large part of many people's social reality, a guaranteed escape route from everyday life. Romance is the magic ingredient of money-making films, Broadway shows, and a vast mountain of mass-market paperbacks. The craving for romance seems overwhelming, and has spawned a multi-million pound industry. Craving for things is always a little excessive, but craving for something as ultimately elusive as romance seems destined to end in disappointment. As with abstract concepts such as luxury or quality, we may have ideas about what would constitute these abstractions for us, but won't everybody's fantasy romance world be different?

Even our fantasies have been moulded by romance, from childhood stories about knights and princesses, through Georgette Heyer and her 'witty, tough, but ultimately melting heroines duelling with fierce, tightly-trousered, emotionally-scarred Earls who were terrifically good at kissing' (to quote the novelist Michèle Roberts), to the latest generation of bold and exciting bodice-rippers with titles like *Sweet Savage Love* and *This Loving Torment*. No wonder every bookseller and librarian knows that the books on the shelves marked 'romance' move the fastest.

What are people looking for? Love? Ah yes, love – an all-embracing (ho ho) concept, often dissected and discussed by moralists, philosophers and theologians. The problem with love is that there is nothing tangible about it, and love is more often a vague ideal than a practice. It seems to change according to its context, so that the love we have for our children takes on quite a different hue from the love we have for the attractive person at a party, not to mention the love of God which for most people totally passeth understanding.

The different hues of love appear to mirror our categories of relationship, which suggests that although love is a valuable concept and a laudable objective, it is of very little use as a theory. I would like to imagine love, between people at any rate, as the state of creativity and joy which includes and surrounds friendship, and then let the word 'love' drop out of the discussion for the time being. Unless we are prepared to question deeply our assumptions and expectations about love, it has too many false connotations and dubious links with romance and conventional sexuality to be particularly useful in looking at the way in which people relate to each other. By seeing how the examination of assumptions about relating can free us to experience love without limiting expectations and therefore without fear, love will ultimately emerge triumphant, but it will be a very different beast from what most of us currently imagine.

So here we are with an interest in intimate friendship, and so far I have questioned the distinction between family, partners and friends, and the necessary connection between friendship, love and romance. What we are left with is the actual phenomenon of friendship, and I think at this point it would be useful to ask what friends are for. Why do we need other people in our lives? It might be useful for you to stop and answer the question for yourself before I list my own ideas.

Different friends fulfil different needs, and we fulfil different needs for them, but here are some possible answers to the question of what friends are for:

❊ A friend is somebody to share things with – from a bar of chocolate or a holiday, or a hug and a cuddle, to passionate sexual intimacy.

❊ A friend is somebody we can trust, trust to understand what we mean, and trust not to tell our innermost secrets to all and sundry.

❦ A friend is somebody we can learn from, more often by comparing experiences and attitudes than the direct learning of skills and techniques, but very important in our overall education.

❦ A friend is somebody that we can teach, particularly if the friend is a child and we are not.

❦ A friend very often acts as a mirror that reflects our thoughts, words and actions, making us more aware of the person we are. Without any reaction to what we say and do from those who we trust and who understand us, our world would become increasingly narrow and self-centred.

❦ We look to friends for affirmation, too. Without the loyalty and support of our friends, life would be very trying – and at times completely overwhelming.

❦ Friends create solidarity. Standing up to authority or a physical challenge can be very difficult without the combined support of our friends.

❦ Our friends are company when we need it. When we choose not to be on our own there they are, often doing nothing more than sitting in the next chair watching television, but there for us when we need them.

❦ Finally, friends are to enjoy, to listen to, to laugh with, to be part of the experience of our lives.

Our friends tend to be people who are like us, partly because we move in circles where we are likely to meet people with similar interests and attitudes, and partly because those interests and attitudes will themselves tend to draw people together. This creates the basis for a shared view of the world, things that you and your friends take for granted and that you don't have to repeat every time you communicate. This makes it easier to move much faster and further in a friendship.

As far as categorising our friends is concerned, we have already seen how difficult it can be to describe our various friendships. A common way of describing friendship is a scale that goes from acquaintance to friend to good friend to best friend. I find most of my friends tend to be borderline cases. I can never be sure what distinguishes a good friend from an ordinary sort of friend, and the categories change as they get cross with me – or remember my birthday.

I am attracted to categories that describe the present state of a relationship, and that are flexible enough to allow changes in the relationship to be reflected in the way we describe them. One such system is that used by Marge Piercy in her inspiring futuristic novel *Woman on the Edge of Time*, where friends can be 'sweet friends', 'hand friends' and 'pillow friends', self-explanatory categories that are clear and direct, and that avoid the exclusive and possessive connotations of words like 'boyfriend' or 'lover'.

Since we relate to all our friends in different ways, and since our ways of being with one friend are constantly changing, it might be most useful, as I've already suggested, to reinstate the word friend to cover all our relationships, and describe our individual relationships in more detail whenever we need to. Thus one person might be a special child friend who I enjoy playing with very much; another may be a work friend; yet another an occasional pillow friend.

Hand friends and pillow friends explicitly include the physical element in relating, and since more open and honest communication is the key to better, more satisfying and ultimately 'safer' intimacy, I particularly like the openness and honesty of a system of classifying friendship which actually describes the current state of play.

Well, openness is all very well if you are clear about your own thoughts and intentions, and honesty is fine if there is some basic agreement about what constitutes reality. As far as friendship is concerned, especially intimate friendship, these are notoriously muddy waters, so let us first look at the way in which we see ourselves and other people.

2

Role Playing

Truth and clarity are extremely difficult concepts to grasp, especially where relationships are concerned. Because our friends are close to us we assume that we know them at least fairly well, understand what they do and know something of who and what they are. We almost certainly know our friends well enough to be able to describe them quite accurately.

When we describe things, we often simplify in order to understand our world more readily. We put things into categories so that we and other people know what we are talking about, and both we and they need to know what the categories mean if we are to make any sense. For instance, if an American met a Londoner and a Liverpudlian, the two Britons would probably both be classified as English, because most Americans don't distinguish between residents of London and Liverpool. People from Britain are not Norwegians or Italians, but all are white Europeans, and as such might well fall into the same category when looked at through the eyes of a black African.

It's the same with descriptions of individual people: we start with broad distinctions, and in order to distinguish one person from another we become more and more detailed. It's interesting, and very revealing, to look at descriptions of people and see which distinctions come first and which ones come later, which are more important and which less.

Here is the tragic heroine of Thomas Hardy's *Tess of the D'Urbervilles*:

> She was a fine and handsome girl – not handsomer than some others, possibly – but her mobile peony mouth and large innocent eyes added eloquence to colour and shape. She wore a red ribbon in her hair.

Here is self-assured Gudrun from D.H. Lawrence's *Women in Love*:

> Gudrun was very beautiful, passive, soft-skinned, soft-limbed. She wore a dress of dark-blue silky stuff, with ruches of blue and green linen lace in the neck and sleeves; and she had emerald-green stockings.

Here is young, sulky Felicity from Iris Murdoch's *The Sandcastle*:

> She was fourteen, very thin and straight, and tall for her age. The skin of her face, which was very white but covered over in summer with a thick scattering of golden freckles, was drawn tightly over the bridge of her nose, giving her a perpetual look of enquiry and astonishment. She had her mother's eyes, a gleaming blue, but filled with a hazier and more dreamy light.

Authors tend to give less space to describing their male characters; they seem to be more active and move before the author has time to describe them in detail.

Muriel Spark's Robinson, from the book of the same name, is seen thus:

> He was short and square, with a brown face and

greyish curly hair.

Robert Stanley, from Elwyn Chamberlain's lurid *Gates of Fire*, is:

Handsome, bisexual, Napoleonically built, and uncouth.

Need we know more? Or does a pattern emerge from these descriptions? I think it does. The first thing we know about the person is their sex; being male or female is the primary and invariably the first distinction. Because our usage of pronouns instantly distinguishes women from men, we know – just one word into each of these descriptions – the gender of the person being described. Where there is no pronoun we have a name; in most languages nearly all names are also gender-specific, so we are rarely confused. The person's maleness or femaleness is paramount.

Then there is a physical description – handsome (both Tess and Robert Stanley, probably the only thing they have in common), beautiful, thin and straight, short and square. The idea of a physical description in a novel is to give us some idea of what the character looks like, and the order in which the details are given reflects the order in which we take in details about people we meet, whether in fiction or in the flesh. I suspect that whoever we asked to describe another person, the order of the details covered would rarely vary much from the following: gender, then age, attractiveness, height and build, face (often with details about eyes, mouth and nose), and clothes.

Most people have two large mental filing drawers labelled 'female' and 'male', and both are the dumping-grounds of quantities of adjectives used to describe people. This hasty and haphazard filing of descriptions is often done because it seems easier not to have to spend too much time doing accurate filing, and means that very many adjectives in common use have acquired pervasive gender overtones. Adjectives are elusive things. For an easy life we often assume that our descriptions *are* reality, when in fact they only reflect the way in which we relate to that reality.

'Handsome, bisexual, Napoleonically built, and uncouth' has to be describing a male character, and, if you don't accept bisexual and uncouth as common adjectives, it works just as well with assertive, reliant, big, strong, hairy or tough. A warm, loving, sensitive, soft, cuddly, dewy-eyed person is difficult to imagine as anything other than a woman. Try to imagine Robert Stanley with a mobile peony mouth and large innocent eyes.

In 1974 an American psychologist called Sandra Bem created a system called the 'Bem Sex Roles Inventory'. Women and men were asked to judge out of a list of 400 descriptive characteristics which of these were more desirable in a man than in a woman, and vice versa. The twenty descriptions that were most often judged to be particularly desirable in one gender were then picked out as being the most accurate defining characteristics for men and women. The results, which are hardly surprising, are as follows:

Feminine characteristics	Masculine characteristics
affectionate	acts as a leader
cheerful	aggressive
childlike	ambitious
compassionate	analytical
does not use harsh language	assertive
eager to soothe hurt feelings	athletic
feminine	competitive
flatterable	defends own beliefs
gentle	dominant
gullible	forceful

loves children	has leadership abilities
loyal	independent
sensitive to needs of others	individualist
shy	makes decisions easily
soft-spoken	masculine
sympathetic	self-reliant
tender	self-sufficient
understanding	strong personality
warm	willing to take a stand
yielding	willing to take risks

The idea is that you see how these qualities relate to you to find out how 'masculine' or 'feminine' you are. It doesn't take much working out to realise that this way of describing people can only exaggerate differences between women and men, since there are no qualities that both are allowed to have. It also shows the shortcomings of not having a flexible filing system. The people who picked the descriptions were asked to respond in a very general and conventional way. Instead of being asked 'Which people do you know who have this quality?' they were asked 'Which of these two vague mental filing drawers would you throw this into?' And they were working within a very structured society where everything from the mass media to the legal system maintains very conventional stereotypes about women and men. No room for change, flexibility and imagination here.

The temptation is now to relate yourself to this imposed pattern and become part of society's norms, thus perpetuating conservative and very limiting attitudes. More contradictions in the Sex Roles Inventory become apparent. There is confusion between being a woman or a man and having feminine or masculine characteristics. Does being self-sufficient and able to make decisions easily really make a women more masculine? Can't men be sympathetic, understanding and compassionate with-

out being feminine? What do 'masculine' and 'feminine'
mean anyway? They obviously don't mean the same as
male and female.

Then there is the pressure on each of us to conform. I'm
a man, and part of me feels I should somehow match up
to Sandra Bem's 'masculine characteristics'. But on her
list I can relate myself to fourteen of her 'masculine'
characteristics and fourteen of her 'feminine' ones. Does
that make me a hermaphrodite or a totally balanced
human being? The generalisations begin to fall apart
when we relate the descriptions to the people we know
well, and realise that nearly all of them could as equally
relate to women or men, blacks or whites, old or young,
princesses or farmers. When we describe somebody, we
are describing one very special and unique person, but
there is a great deal of pressure to use these tools of
language to very conventional ends.

We learn a great deal about any new acquaintance
from their overall appearance, taking in the sorts of
details that novelists (and we, for we are just as imagina-
tive as they are) like to notice. But we also look for less
obvious clues. Just like Sherlock Holmes, we look for little
details that will tell us more about somebody – details of
clothing and hairstyle, jewellery and make-up, posture
and gesture. Not only do we almost instantly know a
person's sex, race, approximate age and something of
their style and idiom; we probably also know their class,
marital status, whether they are able-bodied or have sight
or hearing problems, and whether or not they smoke. All
these things we can take an intelligent guess at very
quickly, often before we exchange a sentence.

First impressions in relating to other people are crucial.
With any potential friendship we have to start somewhere, and those first few minutes will often determine
whether or not the person will continue to engage our
attention beyond our first encounter. At the same time

those first few minutes are precisely the time when many people will be putting on their act (an act designed to appeal to their first impression of us), and we may well be putting on our act (designed to appeal to our first impression of them).

In detective stories clues point to facts. If she was strangled with the butler's scarf, the chances are that the butler did it. The same happens with the clues of a first encounter. If he's wearing a plain ring on the fourth finger of his left hand the chances are that he's married. If a woman and a man are holding hands the chances are that they're partners, and if a young woman is pushing a pushchair she's probably a mother with her baby.

The clues are one thing, and because the non-verbal language of relationship is so well established, from hand-holding and kissing to wedding rings and buggy-pushing, it tells us a lot in those first few minutes during which we decide how we are going to relate to someone. But facts are something else again, and it's very important to distinguish what we know about a person from what we have assumed. The signs are well established, and so are our stereotypes and assumptions. 'Atypical' or 'out-of-character' behaviour often appears to be such because we had assumed something about somebody, rather than because it really doesn't fit in with our previous experience of them. We must all have had an experience of somebody close to us doing something which seemed entirely out of character, but which, as we came to know them better, slotted in completely with our overall picture of them.

Our reactions to apparently 'out-of-character' behaviour often arise because we tend to relate to people in more or less strictly role-defined ways. How would you react to two women holding hands, to a man with his long hair in plaits, to a woman with a shaved head, to a man changing a baby's nappy, to the new acquaintance at a party with whom you are becoming very intimate when you suddenly notice that he or she is wearing a wedding ring?

It's all to do with assumptions, yet without making assumptions we would find it very difficult to relate to the world we live in. If we see a thunder cloud approaching it is only common sense to put on a coat or look for shelter. Similarly if we see two people holding hands, it seems like common sense to assume that they're very together, a couple, and therefore not available for us to relate to closely.

However, it isn't a reasonable comparison, because making a necessary link between hand-holding and unavailability makes some very questionable assumptions. It assumes that two people holding hands have some sort of very special and important relationship, when in fact they may just enjoy holding hands. It assumes that even if they do have a special relationship, then their friendship and closeness are not also available to us. The link between thunder cloud and getting wet is much more direct.

Assumptions exist at all levels of consciousness; many are superficial, and when given the necessary evidence we are quite happy to let go of the assumptions and change our minds. We might have grown up believing all people from Scotland to be mean, but have never made friends with a Scot. Then we meet an open and generous inhabitant of Aberdeen who introduces us to some of their equally open and generous friends. So we drop the assumption and work from the first-hand evidence that the Scots we actually know are friendly and giving.

Other assumptions lie deeper, requiring a lot of convincing before we consider changing them. Many beliefs about the characteristics of men and women are deeply entrenched in our consciousness, not to mention our unconscious. Thus it is not only very difficult to examine them, but almost impossible to recognise them as assumptions at all.

While we might justify our judgements by saying 'that's just the way things are', and even though we might find plenty of first-hand experience to back up our arguments, it is important to remember how often the categories we fit our experience into are as inflexible and conservative as the categories in Sandra Bem's lists. Every time we catch ourselves making unnecessary gender-related connections we limit ourselves; we are working from a belief system based on past experience and assumptions rather than from current first-hand experience.

This tension between working from past generalisations or working from current experience – what some therapeutic and spiritual practices call 'being here now' – gives us much to think about and some difficult decisions to make. It arises because we have to carry on living and making decisions from past experience, yet we are constantly experiencing things that will not fit into our existing mental filing system. Although similar things may have happened before, every experience is different in detail from anything that has gone before.

Psychological and sociological research into the way human beings behave and relate tends to build great structures of generalisation about the ways that people do things. While being useful in the study of large numbers of people, however, generalisations can be very misleading when applied to the behaviour of one individual human being, as we see when we try to relate ourselves to Sandra Bem's averages and find little comparison.

After the link between observation and generalisation comes the even more dubious connection between generalisations and 'normal' behaviour. If you behave according to the averages worked out by social scientists you can be classified as totally normal. If you deviate slightly from the average yet still fit into the categories invented by government departments and the tax system, you will still be considered fairly normal. But everybody must have had an experience of filling in an official form and coming unstuck when the categories given bore no relation to our own situation.

An increasing number of people who choose not to follow the limiting conventions of 'standard' behaviour are finding that major deviations from the average are rarely acknowledged and supported as the free choice of the person concerned. Whether you choose to be a punk, join the Green Party, be a vegetarian, become a single parent, or have a homosexual relationship, the mass of people busy being average would by and large prefer to see you as odd, funny, eccentric, abnormal (or even sick), rather than have their 'normality' affected by your individuality. Nowhere does this apply more than where gender roles are concerned.

Which brings us back to assumptions and expectations – and limitations. To many people the women holding hands are odd enough, but what if they start cuddling on a park bench? And what if you suddenly noticed that the man changing the baby's nappy was wearing a colourful long dress? Or that the women working on the nearby building site had taken off their shirts because they were hot? These harmless examples seem extreme in the context of current expectations of gender-related behaviour, yet everyday public opinion and social pressure are even more restricting, as the father at the playgroup or the single woman at the mixed bar knows only too well.

So why do people do what society expects people of their sex to do?

❀ If you do what people who are like you do, you can be fairly sure of being socially acceptable. If you dress like your friends, do what they do, listen to the same music and watch the same programmes, then you'll have a cosy sense of belonging.

❦ People also do what is expected of them out of fear of what might happen if they did something different. Those who choose to step out of conventional roles are very vulnerable to the judgement of other people. For example, a man who chooses a traditionally 'female' role, like looking after a house and children while his partner goes out to work, has to overcome the fear of what his men friends might think, and the fear that his women friends may ridicule him for being unmanly or sexually naive. Fear is a much stronger reason for the maintenance of social norms than is usually acknowledged.

❦ A crucial reason why people do what is expected of them is that there are economic interests pressurising us to follow their fashions. The manufacturers of make-up, corsetry and lingerie, Y-fronts, after-shave and sexy underwear spend large amounts of time, energy and money persuading us to be conventional, because it is only by supporting and encouraging current beliefs about fashion and attractiveness that they stay in business.

❦ The economic constraints keeping people in their allotted roles are not only those of large organisations and businesses. Many people's fear of stepping out of line is directly related to their fear of losing immediate economic benefits: losing their job, losing a husband who provides financial support, or a wife who provides free domestic services.

❦ Finally, we need to consider what is usually thought to be the most important reason for people doing what is expected of them as women and men – namely, that fundamental and immutable biological differences exist between the sexes which necessitate different behaviour and different social potential. Nobody would deny certain differences – men simply cannot give birth and lactate – but necessary links between vagina, breasts, dresses, long hair and high heels, or between penis, pipe, tie, suit and salary, do not follow as neatly.

So what are the real differences? What would happen if instead of blindly accepting society's conceptions of gender-related behaviour we asked ourselves whether men and women are not so entirely the same thing that the sex distinctions with which our minds are filled might become unnecessary?

3

The Little Differences

The translucent bluish head crowns; another couple of pushes and out slides the new baby. Within the first few seconds we know the answer to that question people have been asking ever since they knew about the pregnancy.

'What is it?' they now ask, knowing what sort of answer to expect. It is such standard practice on hearing about the arrival of a new baby to ask first about its sex that we never dream of wondering why we do it.

The interesting thing is that important though the baby's sex might be to its parents and to us, to the new-born baby itself it makes no difference at all whether it's a girl or a boy. Of course its genitals are different, though it wasn't until the third month of the pregnancy that you could easily have told the sex of the foetus. Even then, the seemingly exaggerated clitoris and labia of a female foetus are difficult to distinguish from the diminutive penis and scrotum of a male.

Until the child starts to find the pleasure of playing with its genitals and begins to get the idea about controlling its excretion, it couldn't care less about its sex organs. Even then it isn't concerned about sex differences – it enjoys the feelings of touch and excretory relief, and its genitals are just part of the whole system that makes the feelings possible.

Yet there is that pervasive genital difference, that tell-tale little sign that divides people into two distinct classes from birth. If God didn't want there to be sexism, why weren't people invented all looking the same between the legs?

It all depends whether you are looking for differences or similarities, and sexual enquiry has been built around the identification and emphasis of all the differences that can possibly be dredged up. If there is a specific factual basis for making distinctions so much the better; hence the magnification of this tiny protuberance or short slit between the legs of babies into a justification for the first and most important distinction we make about people.

In the simplistic and narrow popular culture of sexuality, the protuberance and the hole have become symbolic of all intimate relating. Never mind its concentration on one variety of closeness which leads to all kinds of unjustified assumptions, most people know that what makes sex possible is a sticky-out bit and a nice hole to put it in. This very mechanistic picture of intimacy is reflected in the engineer's familiar 'male' and 'female' nomenclature for bits of metal that fit together. The popular symbolism is pervasive; the sticky-out bit and the hole have become what maleness and femaleness are all about. Nice gentle embracing protective holeyer-than-thou women; nice assertive, penetratingly-astute sticky-out men.

And while this myth was the only one available for most people, our cultural interpretations of biology obligingly concurred. Despite all the evidence to the contrary, it was long assumed that the place where women enjoyed touching and being touched was the inside of the hole – the vagina. It wasn't until very recently that most people discovered that while penetration of the vagina is sometimes enjoyable for many women, the most sexually excitable part of most women's bodies is the clitoris and surrounding area. Like the male penis, it works by having a dense array of sensitive nerve endings and the capacity to swell with blood when excited. Not only is it the most sexually sensitive part of a woman's body, but the manipulation of the area, again as with the penis, is a fairly certain way of creating an orgasm.

With the biological mechanism being the same in women and men, there is little to suggest that there is any fundamental biological difference between female and male orgasm. This is not at all to deny variation in the way that different people experience orgasm, nor to suggest that orgasm is always the aim and result of sexual activity. What I am suggesting is that there is enormous variety between different women's experience of orgasm, and between different men's experience of it, whereas most guides to intimate behaviour stress only the differences between women's experience and men's.

In her fascinating study of human sexuality, *Eve's Secrets*, anatomist Josephine Lowndes Sevely goes one step further. She demonstrates both graphically and convincingly that there is a marked symmetry between male and female sexual organs and sexual responses. The penis and vagina have many anatomical similarities, while the tip of the female clitoris, an organ which extends deep under the skin, is the anatomical equivalent of the tip of the structure within the penis which fills with blood when excited – what she calls the 'male clitoris'.

Thus as far as sexual stimulation is concerned, we *were* all born equal, each with a comforting sticky-out bit to stroke and to help us have orgasms when we want them. Not all the same size, which may help to explain both the preoccupation with the male sticky-out bit and the ease with which the female sticky-out bit can be conveniently ignored, but the potential for pleasure nonetheless.

There was an underlying wisdom that knew this all along – knew that women had sexual feelings that were just as strong and important as men's. Yet this knowledge was in its turn distorted and exploited by male-dominated cultures in one of most disgraceful of supposedly medical disfigurations: the excision of a girl's clitoris, often combined with the sewing together of her vaginal lips to narrow the vaginal opening, a practice still much more widespread than is generally acknowledged.

Of course, little boys suffer too. Especially in North America most male infants have the foreskin cut from their penis, nearly always without anaesthetic. Again it is as though we choose to punish the child for being sexual: circumcision, clitoridectomy and infibulation hurt, providing these children with an early experience of extreme pain in an area we later tell them should be all about pleasure.

Sexual excitement is not the only use for what we call the sex organs; in fact it is not even the main use. From the day we are born until the day we die we urinate at least twice daily, which compares with probably no more than three or four sexual orgasms a week for the most sexually active of us. And here there is quite a noticeable sex difference, at least when we reach the stage of bladder control, for the male human has the wonderful (if rarely mentioned) bonus of directional aim while peeing. Since it is so distinctive it is rather surprising that Freud didn't make a big thing of it, and being one of the few universal sex differences that is biologically incontrovertible could be cashed in on by Desmond Morris and the biological determinists. It certainly keeps the manufacturers of urinals and men's underpants in business by assuming that the biological 'bonus' warrants special treatment, when in fact as we all know that men can manage perfectly well with the same sort of clothing and lavatory fixtures as women.

Sexual dimorphism in urination technique is also noticeable in the supposed freedom it gives men to pee behind any old wall or bush, or even in the open air. I once heard of a young woman who went for two weeks' holiday in the mountains of the English Lake District. Her parents had neglected to teach her how to squat to pee, and she firmly believed that if no public convenience were at hand there was no way in which she could relieve herself. Somebody might see her. Thus, despite the abundant availability of bushes and walls, she held herself in check in the most ladylike way, and developed rather nasty cystitis as a result. End of moral tale, but suffice to say that apart from the added inconvenience of having to pull your trousers down or your skirt up, the freedom to pee in appropriate places is as much a female as a male right.

Enough of these rather rude things. The next little difference is much more socially acceptable – it is the whole process of growing up and developing. At around eleven or twelve years old a girl begins to develop the potential to have babies. Her internal reproductive organs begin to function in an adult way, and she grows breasts with nipples that are usually larger than a man's. This all happens at the same stage at which body hair begins to develop and boys' voices to change – puberty.

Remember that these changes begin around the eleventh or twelfth year of a child's life, before which, apart from the genital difference, there is little physical justification for making any distinction at all between girls and boys. From a voice recording you would have great problems distinguishing between seven- or eight-year-old boys and girls; the boys' hair is only shorter because we cut it; from the waist up there is almost no anatomical difference. If the differences only become apparent at puberty, why is it that we need to distinguish girls from boys from a much earlier age, not only in physical appearance and clothes, but in such diverse things as school subjects, toys and friends?

It must be those hormones. Low though the levels are

during the early years we now know that sex hormones are very important to our health and development. Popular belief has it that there are hormones which are specifically to do with sex – that's why they are called the sex hormones – and that there are hormones found only in men (androgen and testosterone) and hormones found only in women (oestrogen and progesterone), which account for a range of things from ovulation and menstruation to aggression and sex drive. I'm sure research is under way somewhere which will show that hormones also account for why little girls like playing with dolls and little boys with cars and trains.

Hormones are a very recent discovery – the word was only coined in 1904 – and most of the research, especially as far as humans are concerned, is very recent, still in progress, or still to be done. However, let us look at what we do know, starting with the so-called male hormones.

The group of hormones called the androgens (which includes testosterone) have often been seen as the cause of male aggression and sex-drive, and popular accounts such as those of Robert Ardrey (*The Territorial Imperative*) and Konrad Lorenz (*On Aggression*) conclude that there is a direct link between androgen levels and aggressive sexual behaviour in men. The link is a dangerous one to make on several counts.

First, it is a mistake to think that the so-called male hormones are a specifically male attribute. Their names (androgen from the Greek *andros* – man – and testosterone from the male testes) suggest male exclusivity, but there are in fact no hormones exclusive to the male sex, and androgens are created and converted into other hormones (mostly oestrogen) in both men and women, in the adrenal cortex of the brain and in the male testes and female ovaries. In fact, it seems that in both men and women it is the androgens that are associated with sexual arousal, oestrogen and progesterone having little to do with sexual excitement.

Neither are the 'male' sex hormones the only hormones which affect and are affected by 'male' behaviour, particularly aggression. Luteinising hormone, a 'female' hormone, has been shown to be related to aggression in starlings, and progesterone can increase aggression in female hamsters – a 'female' hormone causing aggression in female animals. We hardly need to conduct research to find out that women are also aggressive on occasions, though few studies have been done in this area.

Another problem is that it is almost impossible to measure those aspects of human behaviour supposed to be typically affected by the sex hormones. Aggression or libido are impossible to define within measurable experimental limits. In extreme cases we have no doubt that aggression or lust exist, but how on earth do you measure how aggressive or lustful somebody is? The terms cover such a wide range of very complex behaviour that to organise any sort of experimental scale is pointless.

On the other hand, it is possible to measure hormone levels fairly accurately, so surely all we need to do is watch behaviour patterns as hormone levels change to see what effects hormones have on behaviour. No such luck, I'm afraid, because it is well established that behaviour and environment can drastically affect hormone levels, at least as far as the androgens are concerned. There is little to show that hormones necessarily affect our behaviour at all – it is possible (though unlikely) that changes in androgen level in both men and women are totally induced by our own self-directed behaviour, by such things as physical intimacy or sexual stimulation. As far as hormones are concerned, it is entirely possible that we do it to them as much as they do it to us.

Finally, and most importantly, there is more than enough evidence to show that even if hormones do affect behaviour, it is relatively easy to override the effects of hormones by changing people's circumstances and environment. Human beings are incredibly adaptable, and in experimenting with hormone levels and behaviour it is impossible to ignore things other than hormones that might be causing noticeable differences.

The 'female' sex hormones are quite different in many respects from the androgens. Like androgens, oestrogens are also produced by both men and women; thus there are no specifically 'female' hormones either. Both oestrogen and progesterone, however, have very specific functions in female biology, and not surprisingly there is an intimate link with that area of human experience exclusive to women: ovulation, menstruation, conception, pregnancy, birth and lactation.

The menstrual cycle, which begins at menarche (around twelve years old) and ends with menopause (at around fifty), is an experience common to nearly every woman but one that no man ever experiences. I acknowledge at the outset that I know only what I have read (the greatest debt is to Paula Weideger and her excellent book *Female Cycles*), experienced at second hand, and been told by my women friends.

Several aspects of human female cyclicity stand out as being especially important in the way that people – particularly men and women – relate. The first is simply that men know almost nothing about female rhythms in general, or about the specific rhythms of their women friends. The menstrual cycle is taboo, a mystery, a secret. Understandably so in many ways, since it is one of the few things that women can choose to keep mostly out of male hands. Yet secrecy concerning the menstrual cycle does not assist open and honest communication, and embarrassment surrounding talking about the rhythms of the female body applies even more to men than to women. For a man to talk about women's cycles is almost invariably both embarrassing and considered very rude.

The taboo surrounding the menstrual cycle is incredibly pervasive, and most of the secrecy and fear concerns the 'discharge of a bloody flux' once every three to six weeks. Centuries of alarm concerning the curse of menstruation have meant that the knowledge of this natural and universal development has been passed from head-shaking mothers to frightened and impressionable daughters as a periodic illness that women have always had to put up with. The explanation has often stopped short at the methods by which the awful bleeding can be contained. Menstruation has had a very bad press, and although most men now acknowledge that it is an integral part of female experience, both women and men still tend to be very negative about the 'problems' surrounding it.

The 'horridness' of menstruation has driven female cyclicity underground, to a level of social consciousness where it can only be suffered by the women it hurts and prescribed for by doctors in hushed tones. But although for various reasons cyclicity sometimes involves inconvenience and pain, there are interpretations other than the conventional belief that pain and suffering are an inevitable result of being a woman.

I am sure that we are all aware of times when we work better than at others, times when we feel energetic, positive and ready for anything, and times when we want to hide from the world. I suspect that if we were able more often to do what we felt like, rather than what we had to do to fit in with the timetables of work, school, transport and social engagements, we should feel much happier and more fulfilled. And we should be much healthier. Major problems of organisation, co-ordination and obligation might arise as a result, though these reflect just how little we take human variety into consideration in the way we organise our lives.

Taking people's changing moods and capabilities into

account is much of what female cyclicity is all about. Either we plan and organise projects and jobs and always expect people to fit in with them, or we can be flexible and allow people to live and work according to their own rhythms. And it is this lack of flexibility that often causes women to suffer at the hands of people – mostly men – who cannot acknowledge cyclical changes of mood and ability. According to popular belief, women are moody, irritable, changeable – exaggerated attributes of cyclicity which do not seem to work well within the economic and social structure of Western society. Yet what is wrong is not the ancient 'curse' of cyclicity, but the unnecessary demands of a highly organised timetable, and the unjustified and derogatory exaggerations surrounding the biological fact of cyclicity.

Incidentally, there is growing evidence for cyclicity in men too, and for cycles common to men and women. It is certainly true that if people can follow their own rhythms, once they have grown used to the new freedom it offers, they tend to be both much happier *and* more productive.

Suffering because society's schedules take no account of changing mood and capabilities takes physical form too. The days immediately before a period and the first few days of the period are known to be 'low' days for many women, and the 'female disorder' of pre-menstrual tension has (when acknowledged at all) been seen as a necessary part of women's suffering. Yet where women are free to take account of the natural rhythm of menstruation and take life easier during this period, pre-menstrual tension (and to some extent menstrual pain too) tends to ease.

The cycle is good, natural and positive, and its existence does not make women lower beings than men. If we all worked more closely with our internal rhythms we would find ourselves less stressed and more healthy, and part of this means accepting that menstruation is not a feminine impairment. Having a well-marked cycle is not the same as being physically and mentally incapacitated once a month.

Yet the argument that women are not limited by cyclicity can easily be extended to the point where the cycle is ignored as being unnecessary in the movement towards equality. Women's lives, and to a lesser extent men's lives too, *are* influenced by hormonal changes. Influence is not control, however, and the conventional picture of women as the monthly victims of raging hormonal imbalance is unnecessary and demeaning.

Feelings and desires vary during the menstrual cycle, and in our discussion of relationships it is important to recognise that the cycle also influences women's sexuality. To what extent sexual feelings are affected is difficult to gauge, since not only is it impossible to measure something as abstract as sexual arousal, but it is also difficult to distinguish between changes due to the menstrual cycle itself, and changes due to society's taboo upon menstruation.

Shere Hite's surveys show that if women are asked when during their cycle they are most readily aroused sexually, one third say that they experience no cyclical alteration. Of those who do experience a peak, two-thirds are most aroused just before, during, or just after menstruation. I suspect that most men would be surprised by this, since 40 per cent of men prefer not to be sexually intimate with a woman during menstruation (by comparison only a quarter of women object).

Thus most women experience a noticeable increase in sexual feeling around the time of menstrual flow, an aspect of female sexuality that has been totally obscured by the menstrual taboo, particularly that aspect of the taboo which discourages two-fifths of men from acknowledging any sexual interest in women during menstruation, let alone an increase.

We have looked at the cyclic connection between menstruation and sexuality, but we also need to acknowledge the limitation we put upon female sexuality if we think of it as being 'active' only between menarche and menopause. The difference is often stressed between men with their lack of sexual cyclicity and constancy of hormone levels, and women with their forty-odd 'sexually active' years dominated by hormonal cycles. Yet almost from birth to death a woman experiences sexual feelings and arousal – just as men do. From the early age when a baby discovers its clitoris or penis (and even foetuses have erections), sexual pleasure is literally at its fingertips.

Again the similarities between male and female sexuality far outweigh the differences. Our culture has put women into a sexual double bind of public denial and private horror as far as cyclicity is concerned. As long as we listen to our bodies and not to the so-called experts, we are all potentially free to enjoy our sexuality to the full, acknowledging both our own limitations and capabilities and those of our friends, both female and male.

If the big differences between men and women are not to do with hormones, supposed differences in brain structure are a favourite new theory. It has long been known that of the two hemispheres of our brain the dominant left hemisphere tends to be associated with verbal skills and the right with spatial and non-verbal skills. Because it has been shown that girls tend to develop language skills earlier than boys (we shall come back to the possible reasons for this), a pervasive belief has grown up that the 'left brain' is somehow the epitome of femaleness and the 'right brain' of maleness.

'What is the difference between the brains of men and women?' asks a *Quest* magazine article, obviously expecting to find such a difference. The left-brain/right-brain distinction is one which the esotericists and mystics amongst us are keen to perpetuate – one of those catch-all lumpings-together which are so easy to construct and impossible to prove or disprove. It sounds convincing: intuitive, mysterious, feeling, irrational left-brained feminine women; rational, thinking, logical, cold, right-brained masculine men.

But it simply doesn't work as a biological theory. To begin with the left brain is dominant in all right-handed people, whether men or women. The dominant skills of the two hemispheres show very little difference between the sexes (again the similarities far outweigh the observed differences), and in many cases what would conventionally be called 'male' skills tend to be located in the left brain (like analytical and mathematical skills) and 'female' skills in the right brain (like artistic and musical skills).

So the answer to the *Quest* question is that there is very little fundamental difference between the brains of men and women, and to insist on making unnecessary distinctions not only limits what we believe men and women to be capable of, but undermines those positive and visionary qualities which women, attempting to do things in a more humane and caring way, have spent years cultivating.

Anyone who reads the investigations of sex research must be aware of how little work has actually been done with human beings, and how very often the most amazing results turn out to have come from experiments on rats, hamsters and chickens. My favourite example is pointed out by Barbara Lloyd (in *Exploring Sex Differences*), where one writer – Corinne Hutt – rather naughtily implied that research on androgens and attention level was done on men, when in fact it was done on chicks. Her findings were then quoted by Arianna Stassinopoulos in her book *The Female Woman* where, far from being chickens, the subjects of the research became 'men with high androgen levels, with . . . large chests and biceps . . . and thickset physiques'. We all know about chunky chickens, but this is ridiculous.

Unless we acknowledge that our humanness makes us slightly different from rats and chickens we might as well stop trying to understand ourselves at all. Research into animal behaviour is important if we want to throw light on ourselves and our world, but we must not let the results of such research unnecessarily limit human potential.

Maybe animals are a tempting substitute for people because they are thought to be relatively simple and easy to understand. Trying to find simple solutions to highly complex human behaviour is doomed to failure, and this is why simple biological solutions to the question of sex-role socialisation will not work. In the same *Quest* article, Jerry Levy says that she has 'this almost mystical confidence that true things are simple and elegant and untrue things are complicated and dirty'. This for her justifies an incredible range of male/female distinctions, but in a way I see her point. While I know that people's complex behaviour arises from a very complex mixture of biological potential and environmental moulding, in the end it is the simplest solution that is probably the most elegant and the most true. The simplest solution is that at the most deep and fundamental level all human beings have the same capacity for creative endeavour and fulfilling relationships.

4

Learning to be Limited

Although the sex of the new-born baby is of absolutely no interest to the baby itself, those around it start reacting to its maleness or femaleness from the moment it emerges from its mother.

Traditionally it has been maleness that is considered better all round – a son and heir to carry the family name, a good strong manly baby. In some societies – as Elena Belotti found in the Italian research described in her book *Little Girls* – this preference is very marked, and it is hardly surprising that a male preference at birth goes hand in hand with adult male dominance, the extreme oppression of women, and a markedly sexist society.

Elena Belotti lists many ways in which a child's sex was traditionally predicted by specific signs during pregnancy. If a woman was placid and rosy-cheeked during the pregnancy and took everything easily, the child would be a boy; by contrast, bad temper, crying, paleness and swollen legs suggested a girl. And everybody knew that baby boys were born more easily than girls.

I suspect that for many women in the industrialised West the birth of a daughter no longer has the connotations of failure and negativity that Elena Belotti found in a largely peasant society. Painful contractions during birth are not automatically blamed upon an imagined female foetus, and the mother's feelings during pregnancy are not associated with the prospective sex of the baby. However, I am sure that some women, and more men, are secretly happier when the new-born turns out to be a boy, particularly (though perhaps fortunately this does not apply to most of us) where the inheritance of a title or well-known family name is concerned.

As a result of the growing recognition that women have for far too long been treated as second-class citizens, many women's feelings about the sex of their new-born babies have altered radically. Thirty years ago a boy – especially a first-child boy – was decidedly best, and a woman who kept producing girls was a sorry case. The assumption was (and it was all too often true) that they were trying to have boys, and though the first (and even at a pinch the second) girl baby might have been excusable, to have a third daughter was real mismanagement. And if mothers felt a degree of failure in the non-production of sons, fathers felt it even more acutely.

How different it has been for many mothers – and some fathers too – in the last twenty years, aware of the women's movement and its potential for the new generation of children, especially girls. These parents have found themselves really wanting female children – girls who would grow up to share in the benefits of greater equality. On the other hand, the birth of a son has often been accompanied by very mixed feelings, and the fifty-fifty possibility of having a baby boy has caused many women to think long and hard about conceiving a child. Living with a male child in a very male-oriented society and working with him to counter gender-stereotypes can be very rewarding, as Judith Arcana describes in *Every Mother's Son*, but it also brings the day-to-day issues of oppression right into a woman's everyday life, and can sometimes feel very threatening.

The baby couldn't care less about its sex, but for its

parents and those close to it, its sex revives all sorts of thoughts and memories, making it almost impossible to relate to it in a totally dispassionate and non-judgemental way.

And in the first few days of life the patterns are set. The plastic tag around the baby's wrist, colour-coded pink or blue, leaves no doubt of the baby's sex (heaven forbid that anybody should think of it as *just* a baby), and the colour-coding often extends to cot-blankets, bonnet ribbons, and even dampness detector strips in nappies. Sex stereotyping has started.

For the first few months there is not much for the sex-role traditionalists to latch on to; despite our interest in its sex for reference purposes, babies for the most part steadfastly refuse to prefer pink to blue, or to behave in a particularly male or female way. But that doesn't stop people relating to the baby in ways that they feel to be appropriate.

And here is an important point. The baby may not be behaving in a particularly 'male' or 'female' way, but the people around it have certain expectations, and interpret the baby's behaviour in the way that fits in with those expectations. Thus, for example, there is a strong tendency for adults to attach more importance to the strength and muscles of a male baby – in technical terms, 'to elicit gross motor behaviour'. They are much more likely to handle baby boys roughly and pull their arms and legs vigorously, and to treat girls as though they were more fragile than boys.

The idea of 'male strength' and 'female fragility' has obvious repercussions. Because male babies are encouraged to move more, it is hardly surprising that they tend to be considered as more active; because the expectation is there they become more active, which in turn is considered to be a natural attribute of boy babies and results in more encouragement of 'appropriately' active behaviour.

The complex cause-and-effect of expectation and response is very subtle, so subtle that we tend to overlook it
as an important factor in the socialisation of young children. But though a baby does not respond in an obvious
way to the more subtle messages it receives from its
surroundings, this does not mean that the messages are
not being received. Far from it. By the time a child
reaches the age of two it will almost certainly have a
strong sense of its identity as a girl or a boy. Being
dependent on the reinforcement of its experience by
adults, it will often take sex differences far more for
granted than you or I do.

How does a young child learn what sort of behaviour,
actions and beliefs are expected of it? How does a child
become 'socialised', integrated into society? We must first
return to those things that are done to and for children as
a direct result of their being male or female.

Probably the most obvious difference is the clothes in
which we dress girls and boys. While babygros and
knitted jackets are fairly universal attire for small babies,
by the time the child takes its first steps at least some of
its clothing will usually have been chosen with its sex in
mind. And it is interesting that it is boys who are denied
the variety – girls in pink or blue, frocks and tights or
dungarees, are perfectly acceptable, but a one-year-old
boy in a pink summer frock? Limitations start early.

As the growing child begins to take in its world and
the other people in it, it will try to make sense of the
world by making distinctions, using the new game of
language to articulate these wonderful findings. The child
learns its language from people who already know how
to use it, so the primary distinctions of the adult world
naturally become the early categories of the infant's experience too. The child's 'ma-ma' rapidly translates into
'mummy'; 'da-da' into 'daddy' – it's an observant and
open-minded person who coaxes 'pa-pa' into 'parent',

and expects that to be part of the child's early vocabulary.

And so that the child is in no doubt we tell it that it is a boy or a girl – after all, it has a right to know, doesn't it? We point out 'boy' and 'girl' to the two-year-old – easy words which then get tagged on to children that fit the general description. 'Boy' for a small person with short hair and trousers, 'girl' for one with long hair and a frock. Both hair and clothes, of course, are the result of how adults feel girls and boys should look. No wonder psychologists believe that gender identity is inculcated in most children by the time they are two years old.

Soon afterwards, as experience and vocabulary increase, the child's world embraces 'men' and 'ladies' – an interesting reflection of adult labels – which like 'boys' and 'girls' are usually readily recognisable by their clothes and hair. The stage is set for a totally innocent and unquestioning view of the world in which the division of people into male and female is as fixed and immutable as the timing of *Blue Peter*.

The inevitable result is the sort of conversation that psychologist Dorothy Ullian, in *Exploring Sex Differences*, recorded with a six-year-old:

'A man can do better work than a lady.'
'Why?'
'Because a lady doesn't know so much about working.'
'How come she couldn't learn?'
'Because a man can get more money; he can do more things than the lady because a lady has delicate skin; a man has tougher skin.'
'What makes you think men are stronger than women?'
'Because they were born to be stronger. They were born to be stronger than girls because they do more work than girls.'

How can we expect our children to make anything

different of the world when we work so hard to channel them into conventional behaviour and opinions?

Not long after the discovery of language, children also begin to get the message that some parts of the world are out of bounds, segregated by sex. It may be a while before false modesty and the taboo on nakedness hit with their full force, but the three- or four-year-old will gradually become aware of the way in which public toilets and swimming pool changing rooms are open to half the world and strictly closed to the other half.

Children pick up adult taboos very quickly. Public (and to a large extent private) nudity are discouraged; parents carefully show their five-year-olds how to dress and undress under towels on the beach; a naked two-year-old in most public swimming pools would be frowned upon. They get the message. And goodness knows what would happen if the public should see most little girls' youthful nipples – bikini tops are available for three- and four-year-olds even though there will be nothing to fill them for another ten years.

And we show them how to shut the toilet door (just like a grown up!); the natural elimination of body wastes becomes a private activity, something rather rude. They get the message. The taboo bits of the body that are always covered up become dangerously exciting; jokes about bottoms and willies are exchanged in whispers and giggles.

Well, you may say, it's all very natural. All children go through it: it's an essential part of the learning process. It is certainly part of the process of socialisation into the world that we and our forebears have created, but it is vitally important to recognise that children's supposedly natural reactions are but reactions to attitudes and beliefs that we pass on to them. All too often they limit children, rather than offering them a range of options through which they can grow to their full potential.

Clothes are by no means the only way in which we carefully teach girls the limitations of girlhood and boys the possibilities of boyhood. Children learn much about the world they are to inherit through the medium of the toys they are given to play with.

Most toys are simplified versions of the realities of adult life. As with language, it is important to recognise that although toys are used by children, they are largely the creation of adults who believe that they know what children need. Toys certainly help children to grow up with an understanding of the world, but they also give children a heightened and simplified model of the assumptions and limitations of the adult world. Having outgrown the fluffy bunnies and plastic rattles of babyhood, children start to have toys chosen for them not so much because of their own specific preferences and abilities, but more because adult present-buyers believe that they know the sort of thing that little girls and little boys like. The toymakers and shops are only too willing to oblige, and observations that have been made of the way in which people buy presents for children are revealing, if not altogether surprising.

Traditionally, the main distinction that has been made between toys and games for boys and for girls is that while boys' playthings have been geared to the adult male world of 'important work' and power, girls' toys have reflected the domestic world of home and babies. The stereotypes may not be as marked as twenty years ago, but the toy cookers and hoovers, and the baby dolls that wet their nappies and grow their hair, are still toys that very few people would consider buying for a boy. In the thirty hours that one researcher spent in the toy department of a large furniture store, nobody bought a scientific toy for a girl. The same store had a variety of dressing-up outfits. Boys could be an Indian chief, Superman, a sailor, a racing driver, a policeman or an astronaut; girls could be a nurse, a ballerina, a princess or a bride. Not only did the girls have less choice, but the costumes highlight the differences between the boys' fantasies of power, excitement and speed, and the girls' world of home and service. Added to which adults spent more on boys' toys, spent longer choosing them, and gave them toys (rather than clothes, jewellery and cosmetics) until they were older.

Toys are an important part of a child's training for life, and to start limiting the child's experience before it is five of necessity limits the choices it has in later life. How can the girl who was discouraged from playing with building sets at three ever be expected to grasp physics or engineering at seventeen? How can the boy whose embarrassed parents took his dolls away at four ever hope to be a wonderful and caring parent at twenty?

Things are changing, and there are now many toys on the market that are well-made, safe, and good and creative for all children. And although toy manufacturers and retailers are slow to change, several observers have noticed a marked tendency for those adults closest to a child, especially mothers, to take much more account of its individual tastes and requests than the catalogues, advertisements and packaging of toys conventionally allow.

'He loves knitting,' the mother of a ten-year-old boy confided to researchers John and Elizabeth Newsom (in *The Sex-Role System*). 'It soothes him. He knits tea-cosies, you know, pan-handles, and little gonks and things. He wouldn't knit in front of the boys, I don't think – you know – 'cause he's here on his own you see.'

The mother of a twelve-year-old girl told of her daughter's consuming passion. 'Well you know, she's football mad. We had to buy her a pair of football boots. She had football boots, socks, you know? Last year her teacher turned round and took her to the boys' football team, the man who has the football team. And he turned round and said "You can play better than some of our boys". Oh yes, she's really interested in football.'

The closer an adult is to a child, being sensitive to its needs and requests, the less likely it is that the child will only receive sex-stereotyped playthings, together with the assumptions that go with them.

Authors and publishers of children's books also often seem to have a very dull and stereotyped view of the world. This is a pity because, both before school and particularly while at primary school, children take what they read to be the way the world should be, even when their direct experience of how the world is is entirely different.

Many children still learn to read with the help of a reading scheme, and in 1974 Glenys Lobban looked at the six most popular British reading schemes. She found that they rigidly divided human activity into either 'masculine' or 'feminine', with very few characteristics common to both. As portrayed in the schemes the boys had a wider choice of toys, were doing a much wider range of activities, and nearly always took the lead in activities that involved both sexes. Perhaps even more importantly, since children are always looking for adult models, adult roles portrayed in half or more of the six schemes showed markedly different possibilities for men and women. Women were mostly mothers, aunts and grannies. If they were allowed to work, then they were teachers and shop assistants. By contrast, men appeared in fifteen different roles – driving trains and buses, fishing, farming and building among them.

Not one of the 179 stories Glenys Lobban looked at showed a man doing housework or cooking anything other than a cup of tea (except when Mum unfortunately had to go into hospital to have a baby). Dad was always driving *his* car – only one book showed a woman driver – and the schemes abounded in pictures of Dad reading the paper or watching the television while Mum made the dinner and washed it up, often with the daughter helping.

Though the last two decades have seen the publication of many children's books that do portray girls and boys in more egalitarian and less limiting roles, the books from which our children learn their language have changed remarkably little. Carolyn Baker and Peter Freebody's 1989 study, *Children's First School Books*, reveals that early reading material is still noticeably skewed in favour of men and male activities. The word 'boy' or 'boys', for example, appears three times for every twice that 'girl' or 'girls' appears. There are nearly twice as many male proper names as there are female ones. They also document what they call 'the cuddle factor' – the word 'girl' is far more likely than 'boy' to be preceded by the word 'little', while boys are the only children to be described as 'brave' and 'naughty'.

For most children, real life is nothing like as stereotyped as the early reading books suggest, but the authority of the printed word and the pictures in the book are difficult for a child to deny. These days most children's worlds include single-parent families, people of races and backgrounds other than their own, and men who are able to cook more than a teabag. In this context it is incredibly limiting to learn to read with a reading scheme in which two-child suburban middle-class nuclear-family sex-stereotyped values are the only model.

While the majority of children's books are still extremely conventional, a range of alternatives to sex-stereotyped material is gradually becoming available. From excellent picture books by Stan and Jan Berenstain and Shirley Hughes to exciting and provocative stories for young adults by well-known authors like Rosemary Sutcliff and Ursula LeGuin, children can now read about women warriors and astronauts, and men who wash up and babysit.

The range of alternatives for girls is increasing most rapidly (largely a result of the limited options previously available), and this is particularly good news in the light of the growing amount of research showing that girls tend to develop their reading skills earlier than boys, with a large majority of girls learning to read before they go to school (leaving a larger proportion of boys to learn at school with the aforementioned reading schemes). This tendency has been biologised into a supposed sex-related ability of girls to develop verbal skills earlier than boys, without taking into account the pervasive influence of expectation. Little girls are often read to more and talked to more (reading and talking being considered sedentary rather than active skills – 'female' rather than 'male'). They are expected to learn to read and write more easily than boys and, since words and books are fun, little girls readily fulfil the expectation. To fulfil a challenging and exciting expectation hardly needs a biological explanation.

If books often provide excessively stereotyped models, television is usually even worse. Just to give a small example, one study of television commercials in the USA showed that men outnumbered women three to two, and in the two-thirds of adverts that had a narrator extolling the virtues of the advertised product, 92 per cent of them were men – smooth-talking, authoritative, powerful men. The remaining 8 per cent of woman narrators all appeared in commercials advertising 'women's products'. Men told women how to wash shirts cleaner, how to look after their children, which dishwasher to buy. It seems that women can't tell men anything.

Once the child becomes part of the school system, all sorts of other pressures work to maintain them in their allotted sex roles. Clothing often becomes institutionalised in school uniform, and every item of apparel takes

on gender characteristics. The early dichotomy of toys
and games is upheld at every turn, especially when the
distinction starts between 'girls' sports and 'boys' sports.
In the playground, boys' games often involve running,
kicking and shouting, while the girls skip or play house
or school quietly in the corner. Boys and girls playing
together is a rarity, often enforced by the teasing and
taunting of children who cross the gender barrier. It is
hardly surprising that researchers John and Elizabeth
Newsom found that of the eleven-year-olds they talked to
who had a best friend, 98 per cent of best friends were the
same sex as the child they were talking to.

. In the classroom the quietness and prettiness of little
girls receive praise. Boys are expected to fight and be
competitive – they oblige by rising to the teacher's expectations. Girls are good and obedient, easier to teach. Boys
are louder, ask more questions, and nearly always have
their hands up first. It has widely been assumed that this
is part of the natural order, but at last some teachers are
beginning to question the system that encourages success
in boys and often, in very subtle ways, allows girls to fail.

Limitations are built into the school curriculum for
most children at an early stage and, together with stereotyped messages from teachers and the wide world, by
secondary school the differences in expectations and performance between girls and boys have become very
marked. The most obvious is in the range of subjects that
boys and girls study. While legislation may make it
possible for children to cross previously gender-demar-
cated boundaries, very few do so.

One stated objective of the recently introduced National Curriculum in British schooling is to ensure that all
children should have a good foundation in maths and
science as well as in language. A recent study called
Gender, Primary Schools and the National Curriculum, by
Alan Smithers and Pauline Zientek, suggests that policy

changes alone will have little effect until society's attitudes start to change. 'It will take more than the National Curriculum to change attitudes and expectations,' responded one teacher. 'Although children at school cook and sew, perform scientific experiments and build with saws, wood and boxes, they still regard sewing at home as mummy's work, while woodwork is for daddy.'

Physics, chemistry, metalwork and technical drawing remain overwhelmingly 'male' subjects; languages, biology, commercial subjects and 'homecare' are the girls' stronghold. Few children are encouraged to cross the threshold into non-conventional subjects by their career-minded teachers and advisors and children mostly prefer the company of their gender peers when the choice is available. It is often assumed that children choose subjects because they enjoy those subjects. However, after we have spent five or six years telling them that the subject is not gender-appropriate and that it won't help them find a job, they can no longer be expected to make a genuinely free choice. It is hardly surprising that fewer than a thousand British teenage girls (compared with over 150,000 boys) choose to do technical drawing, woodwork or metalwork each year.

Another limitation, which again affects girls more than boys, is the general absence of female models in school textbooks. When they are there they are often insignificant, subordinate, or merely decorative. In a study of bias and insensitivity in primary mathematics materials entitled *Everyone Counts*, Fran Mosley points out a typical textbook example which states baldly that 'Men use force when they push a car'. What then do women use? Social science texts – geography, history and social studies – are particularly bad in this respect, often rendering the female half of the population invisible.

The small amount of research that has been done on the way in which teachers work with children in mixed-sex classrooms shows fairly conclusively that with very few exceptions the main focus is always on the boys in the class. Boys more often seek the teacher's attention (and get it), and are much more ready to answer questions and offer advice. They tend to sit at the front, and because they are more demanding they are more often asked to demonstrate examples and look things up. The girls have learnt that this is just how boys are; girls tend to be shyer, more compliant and willing to please. As their reward for being less demanding, girls receive less attention.

Girls may receive less attention in most academic subjects, but most people agree that schools exist not only to teach academic subjects. School is also the setting in which children receive much of their early experience of relating to other children, both singly and in groups, yet the art of relating is a subject in which neither girls nor boys receive much attention. I believe strongly that everybody should learn as early as possible how to be warm, loving and supportive to other people, and how to overcome the barriers that stop them relating to other people as equals. Important as it is, however, learning to relate openly and warmly is in most schools the one thing that is not only *not* taught, but is actively outlawed.

By their mid-teens, children have been taught that physical closeness, especially between the sexes, is definitely not OK. Hugging and kissing is only for babies and lovers; if you do it, it can only mean you're going steady with someone, and if you get caught doing it by teachers or parents it'll mean real trouble. The only education that most children get about physical contact with their friends is the standard 'sex education', covering human reproduction, contraception, venereal disease and, usually for the girls only, menstruation.

For a start, the actual information that is given is often either wrong or incomplete. Anja Meulenbelt's sex education book, *For Ourselves*, gives several examples of diagrams of the 'female reproductive system' (to call anything sexual or genital would be too risky) which ignore the existence of the clitoris. As well as being misleading, the biology that supposedly constitutes sex education is very mechanical. It's little wonder that young people are confused by sex when it's presented as a purely physical experience akin to sneezing or swallowing. Feelings and fears hardly get a look-in.

Young people aren't fooled by this whitewash. 'Part of the reason I've felt powerless in the past is because sex education is so bad,' writes one young woman. 'It's all so biological – there's very little about contraception, abortion is all hushed up, and no one ever mentions pleasure. All the bits they miss out at school, like masturbation or homosexuality, you learn from your friends in a sort of sneaky, dirty way. There should be a lot more discussion at school about sexuality, perhaps in single-sex groups, but unless teachers themselves are open-minded it would be a waste of time.'

The way that sex education is taught in most schools (though there are some notable exceptions) is based on one very conventional and mechanical way of being physically intimate, together with its dire consequences of unwanted pregnancy and terrible disease. As well as teaching that shared sexuality is something to be frightened of, standard sex education unintentionally reinforces the belief that there are only two ways of being with other people – distant and aloof, or in bed making love. How can we expect children to learn about the pleasures of warm closeness, stroking, hugging, kissing, cuddling, holding and being kind and loving to each other, when we react with horror to any suggestion of physical closeness, and give them no education at all in how to experience the variety of ways of relating?

I can just imagine the reaction of most adults to the

teaching of massage in school, or mixed sex saunas and showers. As for a class where the pupils were encouraged to touch and hug each other – well, you know what that would lead to! Innovations like this would have to be introduced very carefully and sensitively; it certainly couldn't be done overnight. Sex-role conditioning of both teachers and children, even that of young children, would make sexual harassment an ever-present threat, and the current moral climate would certainly not support such a move.

But the problems that adults have with ideas like this are largely due to their own frustrations and fears, and until we are clear with children and young adults that closeness and warmth and touch and support are essential to health and happiness, we shall continue to be frightened and frustrated by knowing how nice it is to be close to people, but being so scared that we never do it. If anyone is hoping that the majority of current sex education is helping children to grow up into caring, supportive adults with a balanced outlook on closeness and sexuality, the hope is a vain one. At present the education of children in this vital area of experience is, with very few exceptions, pathetic.

The notion that closeness and warmth are wrong and bad is a terrible belief to instil in our children, and probably one of the biggest disservices that our education system does to them. If we didn't spend so much time teaching children – especially boys – how to be self-centred, isolated and competitive, they wouldn't have all that fear and separation to unlearn later on. Surely we should encourage children to be warm and loving, caring and co-operative, and help them to express their feelings about physical intimacy in a safe and supportive setting. If this kind of support were commonplace, children wouldn't have to deal with such agonies in their teens, and wouldn't later on have to relearn sensitive and loving closeness with their boyfriends and girlfriends with no support, no help, and usually with pointed disapproval.

5

Should I or Shouldn't I?

In much advice about sex, especially for young people, it is assumed that the fundamental question when thinking about sexual activity is 'Should I or shouldn't I?' This seems a singularly pointless question without asking what it is we are talking about: should I or shouldn't I *what*? This is where the embarrassment usually starts, because people not only don't much like talking about *it*; *it* is very private, very rude, and very painful, and our culture and language just don't have polite ways of dealing with *it*.

It, of course, is sex. Should I or shouldn't I engage in sex? But the question is nothing like as simple as it looks.

To begin with it implies that we have a choice whether or not to have sex in our lives at all. We can, if we choose, not allow our naked body to come into contact with anyone else's, and we can choose not to sleep in the same bed as someone else. Assuming that we understand the necessary mechanics (and sex education often fails even here), we can choose not to masturbate, or not to have intercourse with anybody. The various forms of celibacy, particularly the recent interest in feminist celibacy (a more or less conscious solution to a seemingly intractable situation) certainly stop other people being intimate with our sexuality, but, even if we go to the lengths of cutting off our sexual parts and becoming a hermit, nobody can live a totally sexless life. Our sexuality is as much an integral part of our being as any of our senses and thoughts, and just as impossible to separate out from our total existence.

The question also implies that we know what we mean by sex, and can control our relationships consciously to include or exclude sex from them. Since sexless people do not exist, any involvement between two people has the potential for a sexual encounter. Relating obviously includes much more than sexuality, but to ignore the sexual element in any encounter is unrealistic, and doesn't help any deep understanding of the relationship. When we are trying to work out what is sexual and what isn't, we can create as many limits as we like; we can say for example that nothing specifically sexual is involved until physical contact is made. But we know perfectly well that it is very easy for people to relate sexually without touching each other; certain ways of talking and looking and smiling can create a situation that few people would not consider to be sexual. And it's equally possible for people to be physically close without any intention of sharing sexuality. All closeness includes the possibility of sexual closeness, but closeness does not *have* to include sex.

If sex is such an integral part of our existence, then it is inherent in the whole way we relate to other people. Are there clear answers to questions like 'Is it sexual to kiss a friend on the lips?' or 'Is it sexual to lie naked with somebody else?'

Sex is at least implicit in all relationships, but is there behaviour that is always and only sexual? The sex manuals are again pretty unanimous that there is an ultimate *it*, an *it* that is incontrovertibly sexual.

It is the very specific process of the insertion of the

erect male penis into the vagina of a woman, followed by movements which bring the man at least to orgasm – the activity known variously as 'making love', 'having intercourse', 'having sex', or, least ambiguously, as fucking. Fucking is almost always assumed to be the ultimate goal of all other intimate behaviour, often tellingly lumped under the term 'foreplay'.

Sexual activity has traditionally been seen as a sort of downward slide from socially acceptable public behaviour between two people – the sort of thing that nobody would object to – to totally private behaviour that would be most embarrassing, if not quite scandalous, to most people if they were witness to it. At some point on the scale, and the point varies from participant to participant and situation to situation, behaviour 'turns' sexual.

Favourite crossing-points these days, though they are often quite arbitrary and the result of the quest for definitions of *it*, include the open-mouthed kiss, the hand under the clothing, or the long meaningful hug.

For several reasons I believe that this way of looking at sexuality is doomed to failure in our exploration of new ways of getting close to other people. As we shall see in Chapter 12, the first thing to remember is that our language often limits us into very inflexible ways of looking at our behaviour. It's difficult to tell which comes first – the way of behaving or the way of describing it – but it is clear that the accepted continuum of sexual behaviour from first sexual feelings to inevitable climax is firmly entrenched in our thinking about sexuality.

Most of our sexual vocabulary is built up around a general belief that there is one, and only one, normal course for sexual behaviour, a progression so much part of our cultural imagination that alternatives are difficult to imagine. The almost universal expectation is that orgasm follows penetration follows foreplay like Sunday morning follows Saturday night.

This way of looking at sexuality assumes that closeness between a woman and a man is always doomed to a standard progression (though 'standard decline' might describe it better) towards more and more intimacy, with the inevitable expectation being the fully fledged fuck, and equally inevitable feelings of failure if the ultimate goal is not reached.

With the weight of cultural expectation behind the myth, the alternatives to the 'normal' sexual progression are hard to imagine, but alternatives there certainly are. In the new world of AIDS, a few lone voices are beginning to suggest that 'safe pleasuring' can take a multitude of different forms. Without clear descriptions and enough experience to prove these assertions, however, the 'standard model' of sex will continue to prevail. We have already seen how a seemingly simple suggestion like 'mutual masturbation' can be misunderstood; another public AIDS awareness campaign suggests – without any further explanation – that 'frottage can also be fun'. Have you tried looking up 'frottage' in a standard school dictionary?

Exploring the alternatives needs at least two important understandings: that any sort of closeness, including sex, can be enjoyed for its own sake without the need of sexual goals; and that there is nothing about sex (with the exception of the final stages of orgasm) that is uncontrollable.

Not that intercourse and orgasm aren't good things to share and experience. Sensitive and aware penetration (or enclosing if you look at it from the vagina's point of view) and shared orgasm can bring people together like almost nothing else. The intimacy that comes before and after it can be equally exciting and passionate. It's just that sexual intercourse is by no means the whole story. There are hundreds of ways of being close to somebody and sharing loving feelings, and only some of them need to include intercourse and orgasm. Nearly all the models we are shown in print and on the screen deny the other possibilities.

Our culture has an enormous investment in persuading us of the supposed normality of the standard progression of sex. But it's simply not true that some sorts of sexual behaviour are more natural than others. Some ways of behaving are certainly more hurtful and oppressive than others, and experimentation does not excuse violence and insensitivity, but – as we shall see – the sensitive exploration of physical closeness can only improve the way we relate to one another.

Though closeness and physical contact are usually received and given during sexual sharing, it is important to remember that intimacy and touch do not *have* to be the prelude to a sexual future. As we shall discover in later chapters, to suggest that shared intimacy has to involve pain and regret is to deny our innate intelligence and ability to choose for ourselves. Because of the confusion and silence surrounding intimacy, however, it is all too easy for our real needs for closeness and touch to become unruly cravings, demands by one person of somebody else who doesn't want to participate, or assumed to be natural urges that cannot be controlled. We don't have to deny our needs, but we do need to be as clear as we can about what we want.

So what are the necessary elements for a close encounter of the best kind?

First, it helps to be in constant touch with what you are feeling about the encounter. Because of our indoctrination with the myth of progression, the question we often find ourselves asking is 'What is going to happen next?' It's a reasonable question in some circumstances, as when someone asks you what you are doing tonight, but wondering what's going to happen next so often spoils our enjoyment of what's happening now. Instead of asking

'What's going to happen next?', the appropriate question is more often 'Am I enjoying what's happening now?'

Imagine yourself at a party where you have met somebody who is very attractive, and who obviously finds you attractive too. You are talking, getting close to each other, enjoying one another's company. You're hugging each other, stroking each other occasionally, and it's feeling very pleasant. Yet you keep wondering what's going to happen next, torn between the pleasure of the moment and the anticipation of the future. This is probably particularly true if you are a man with a woman, because men are told that their role is to initiate things, and that sexual conquest is what closeness is all about.

Anticipation certainly has a positive side, but it is very easy to play down the nice things that are happening now for the supposedly nicer things still to come. If you asked yourself what you'd like to happen next, the honest answer might well be 'More of the same, please', especially if you are a woman with a man, for women have often grown passively used to not having their wants listened to or their sexual preferences understood.

In sexual behaviour it is usually tacitly understood that what happens next is vitally important, if only to somehow confirm what has already happened. How can I be sure he loves me if I don't let him do the next thing on the list, and how can I be sure he'll know that I love him if I don't reciprocate with the standard response?

Part of the problem of what happens next is the question of who's in control of the situation. As we have seen, the socialisation of men and women has taught that men are dominant and women submissive – that in most heterosexual encounters a man will 'naturally' decide what is going to happen, and control the situation in order to make it happen.

We'll come to power and threat again in a later chapter, but it seems obvious to me that shared intimacy can only work well when it is clearly accepted that both participants can say what they want and what they like, and have their preferences heard and acted on. Simply put, the best intimacies will be between people who are in constant touch with what they feel about the situation, and who accept each other as equals.

A second element of successful shared intimacy is to forget many of our received ideas about what is sexual and what is not. I strongly believe that sexologists and the collective cultural imagination have closed to us a lot of very necessary contact and intimacy between people by calling it sexual, and thereby making it private, scary and treacherous. A lot of not-specifically-sexual closeness gives us sexual feelings, but we can always choose to feel and talk about the feelings, and cry or laugh or shout if we need to, without *doing* anything sexual.

Looking for the boundaries, asking 'Has it turned sexual yet?', doesn't help a lot if you and the other person are obviously enjoying yourselves in a conscious way. It is nearly always much more productive to ask 'Is what is happening what I want to happen, is it what the other person wants to happen, and am I doing my best not to hurt anybody?'

Touching and being touched by other people is a very important human need, and at the same time is probably the most difficult of basic human needs to differentiate from what most people consider to be a necessary and inevitable overture to further intimacy. The pleasure of being stroked, massaged, or just held, is obviously a pleasure in its own right, but for most people there is very little close physical contact other than with children and lovers. Yet there are often people in our life with whom we would sometimes like to explore physical contact without the obligation of total intimacy.

A lot of the problem is knowing what to do with our sexual feelings. Close physical contact is often accompanied by sexual arousal for both men and women. While sexual arousal is probably experienced by women and men to much the same extent, the biological fact of an erect penis, a phenomenon that is difficult to ignore during physical intimacy, has been used in the lore of sexology as yet another indicator of male sexual dominance. The less obvious external symptoms of arousal for women have assisted the widespread belief that women are sexually aroused to a lesser degree and less often than men.

The mythology has led to an enormous difference between what women think they need to do with their feelings of sexual excitement and what men think they need to do with theirs. Women have in general been taught to ignore their sexual feelings, or to sublimate them in romantic fantasy. Most men have learned that if they are sexually aroused, their penis is telling them that the person who has triggered the reaction is a prime candidate for shared sex.

Whatever the thoughts that accompany sexual arousal, the fact is that owners of sexual feelings very rarely feel safe enough to deal with them directly and honestly. We don't usually talk about being aroused because, in our society, to talk about our own sexual feelings or to make it clear that we have noticed somebody else's, implies an overt sexual interest in the person jointly responsible for the arousal. So we just ignore it and wait for it to go away.

If you have ever read a naturist magazine like *Health and Efficiency*, you may have noticed that one of the perennial questions from male budding-but-shy nudists is 'What would happen if I was sexually aroused and had an erection while we were all naked together?' Part of the answer is that arousal does not automatically accompany nakedness, although for men not used to taking their clothes off in company the penis sometimes takes a while to adjust to new circumstances. But the assurance that men can be in mixed naked company without an erection, and even photographs proving the point, does not help the man who is aroused sexually to handle his own and other people's reactions.

The simple fact is that arousal need not imply any additional sexual intention at all. When we choose it to be, arousal can only and simply be arousal and nothing more, *and* something we can celebrate by talking about it and sharing our experience. We can enjoy the feeling in its own right.

Breaking the cultural link between physical contact and sexual arousal will not necessarily make arousal go away – it may well do the opposite. If we can feel safe to be sexually aroused in the knowledge that we can enjoy it for its own sake, we may find it happening more often. To celebrate ourselves as the owners of sexual feelings without having to extend the performance is not easy, because we are not used to doing it, but there is little chance for us to be sexually honest with each other if we can't even tell somebody else what our body thinks it wants when its sexuality is tickled.

The fact that some sorts of touching by some people arouse us sexually suggests that there are some sorts of touching that are intrinsically sexual and some that are not. Again, I would suggest that it's the thinking that something is sexual that makes it so, and that the distinction between 'sexual' and 'non-sexual' touching is as much to do with our expectations and past experience of closeness as with biology.

It is true, for instance, that our lips are very sensitive, but not so much more sensitive than the rest of our skin that kissing somebody else on the lips is unquestionably more sexual than kissing them on the cheek. The tongue is not so much more sensitive than the lips that kissing with your mouth open is always in a different realm again of sexual experience. The progression of sexual encounter has only acquired the significance it has because we have given it that significance. If we can be clearer about our needs and intentions, we can choose to clarify the significance of our actions by agreeing with the other person that we want it to be different. We *can* be entirely clear that what we are offering is a massage with no deliberate genital stimulation. We *can* agree that we shall sleep in the same bed and cuddle, but without having orgasms or intercourse.

We need to understand that different sorts of physical intimacy can be enjoyed and celebrated completely and only for themselves. Kissing need only be kissing, and even genital stroking can be that and nothing more or less. Although maybe a rare and strange experience, the enclosure of an erect penis in a warm vagina can be thoroughly enjoyed for its own sake, with no expectation of orgasm.

In this context, 'safer sex' takes on a new dimension. Instead of AIDS precautions taking the form of standard-sex-with-condom-and-without-discussion, you can talk about what sorts of intimacy you feel comfortable with. The only way in which sexual encounter can be what we choose it to be is if we can communicate about it clearly with the person we are sharing it with. This sounds rather clinical, since so much of the progress of intimacy is traditionally non-verbal, but the freedom and innovation that follow from clearly shared feelings and desires more than reward the initial risk.

This leads directly to a third element of fulfilling intimate encounters, an element that might be called 'the inner game of sex'. Sex is not something that happens only in the genitals – far from it. Like most behaviour, it 'happens' mostly in the head, with your whole body involved in playing the game directed by the brain. Shared intimacy is a very exciting game, a subtle interplay of words and actions between the participants. Messages are put out – touches, questions, the sharing of feelings – to see how the other person responds. The reciprocation of the communication creates a situation where both people know that more closeness is totally appropriate.

What helps enormously while this is happening is open communication. The brain works mostly with words – the 'inner game of sex' is a long monologue going on inside your head. This is a monologue that we have learned to keep to ourselves because sex is considered to be a very private thing. But it usually takes two people to have a relationship, and especially in the early stages of closeness it helps enormously to turn the internal monologue into words that the other person can hear. It is only in this way that we can find out what the other person is experiencing, and the only way they will know what is happening for us. This goes directly against an ingrained belief that the best intimacy and shared sexuality is silent and thereby meaningful – the silence may mean one thing to you, but it's very unlikely that it will mean the same to your partner.

It is impossible to overstress the importance of clear communication, since for so long it has been the general belief that the passion of true and meaningful love is beyond words. As we shall see in the chapter on language, it is certainly true that the language of relating is often very vague and indirect, which doesn't help clarity. Talking often seems to detract from the sexual experience, and can sometimes be an embarrassed substitute for deep feelings and aware physical closeness, but sharing feelings and desires clearly and sensitively during sexual closeness can be enormously exciting. Breaking through the fear and politeness to real, open and clear communication in close relationships feels difficult, but I have found it to be one of the most liberating experiences of

my life, a reward that always far outweighs the tempo-
rary scariness and unease of knowing that something
needs saying and being too frightened to say it.

The myth of the meaningful silence often combines
with the myth of the feelingless man doubly to frustrate
open and clear communication in a heterosexual relationship. Many women have experienced a blank wall of
non-communication in a man they are relating with, often
at just the time when the woman is trying to be very clear
and honest, making it more difficult for the man to hide
his true feelings and desires. He feels cornered, with
silence (or walking out of the room) his only defence, but
this is one of those situations where the only way out that
serves both people is for the silent partner to do exactly
the opposite of what they feel like doing – talking. The
only other alternative is to agree not to communicate,
though this seems hard on the one – usually the woman –
doing most of the work.

There are a couple more important aspects of communication, both to do with asking for what you want.
Because sex – meaning intercourse – has all too often
become the synonym for physical closeness, it is often
difficult to decide exactly what it is that you do want
when the general feeling is one of 'wanting sex'. For men
especially this is a hard one to disentangle, since the male
sexual myth of physical closeness equalling sex is amaz-
ingly rampant. A woman can usually ask for a hug quite
easily, at least from another woman or a close male
friend, but many men find the concept of asking 'only' for
a hug difficult to imagine: 'I don't want to start something I can't finish,' explained one man to Bernie Zilbergeld, the author of *Male Sexuality*. Yet even such a strong
belief can be counteracted by continuing to ask ourselves
what it is that we *really* want every time we think we
want sex. A list of possible candidates might be: a long
talk, our hair stroked, our back scratched, a ten-minute

cuddle, a massage, to have somebody say how much they love us, a close hug, to masturbate. The list is endless, yet a tacit belief in the universal desire to fuck automatically wipes out all the alternatives.

My other point about asking for what you want is to do with remaining positive rather than just saying what you don't want. Where men are supposed to initiate and control sex, women are often put in the position of silently receiving physical attention, saying nothing during the good bits and objecting to the scary or painful bits. This ties in directly with most men's fears about rejection and not performing properly, and assists the closeness not one iota. When both people can say clearly what they like and what they want, there is much less room for things happening that one person doesn't want or like. It takes courage to take on the twin myths of passionate silence and male performance at the same time.

Of course, saying clearly what needs to be said constitutes only half of the necessary communication between two people. The other half is open and attentive listening, and most people aren't very good at listening. Our culture teaches us that it's often more important to get in our own say than to listen to somebody else, and that conversation is a battleground. The person who can talk loudest and interrupt the most successfully is the person who gets listened to.

If we are serious about communicating clearly in close relationships, part of our commitment has to be the willingness to listen well and attentively to our partner without interrupting or contradicting them. This can be a very difficult thing to learn, especially for men, who have not only been taught to communicate very competitively, but have also learned that what men say, especially when communicating with women, has to be right. If a woman says she feels threatened by a man's sexual advances, for instance, the immediate male response might well be to interrupt with 'Don't be silly, you can't be feeling threatened. I'm not threatening you.' When people are allowing themselves to be vulnerable by expressing their feelings, however, the last things they need to hear are that what they are saying is so unimportant that it can be interrupted, that they are stupid, and that they are not feeling something they so definitely *are*.

It is very exciting and challenging to move towards closeness in a very aware way, yet it is territory where very few people have been before. As you explore intimacy in this way you will often find yourself in new situations that you know you have chosen, but that are so like similar times in the past when things went completely wrong that you forget that this time you are in control.

You may, for example, be lying in bed with somebody of the other sex, stroking and being stroked, feeling warm sexual feelings, and also knowing and being clear that you and your partner have talked about what you want, and have decided that you don't want intercourse or to have an orgasm. But it's all feeling really good, and it seems as though before you know where you are penis and vagina have somehow become engaged.

It may be that this now feels entirely appropriate, and when you check out what you both want you agree that it is. After all, everybody has the right to change their mind. If it isn't, however, even though it contradicts everything you have learned about sexual closeness, you *can* choose again to return to the safe cuddles without the threatening penetration. Situations like this can feel very difficult – dealing with them needs practice – but the freedom and clarity that follow can create deep understanding and trust between lovers.

It feels even harder to deal with situations where just one of the partners feels as though they've done something they had previously chosen not to. It's easy at times like this to feel that you've failed and let the other person down, especially if you've done something that the other person has specifically asked you not to. In heterosexual encounters this happens most often to men, because the initiation of intimate behaviour by men is such a deeply ingrained practice, and because it goes against a lot of what we have learned about sexual behaviour from the sex experts. The sex manual says that a woman likes having her clitoris stroked, so why is she saying she doesn't want it? And however much I understand what she wants, my hand keeps straying towards her genitals. Surely she'll start to feel like it soon. Oh no, why is she crying? Why is she getting angry? It's not fair; I'm only doing my best.

It's really important at times like these to know that you can still listen, still be sensitive, and still choose. Even though you haven't done what you intended to, you *have* done your very best in strange and risky circumstances. And it's important, though very difficult sometimes, to communicate all your thoughts and feelings to the other person, so that they know exactly what is happening for you.

For nearly everybody, sexual encounter has had a great deal of pain and grief associated with it, which makes it very difficult to believe that intimacy can ever be joyful and painfree. The roots of the pain lie deep in our individual pasts. Because most of us grew up in a very repressed society, we never received much of the love and touching and stroking that every child wants. We were told in so many ways that sex is private and disgusting and dirty; how could it ever be beautiful and open, delighted in and celebrated? It takes a great deal of self-examination and awareness to know that we can enjoy and share our sexual feelings, and the rediscovery of long-repressed feelings will probably be accompanied

by quantities of tears and a great deal of anger. It takes a
lot to go through all that, and *know* that our lives can only
be better at the end of it all.

6

The Sexual Web

The ability to love and be loved by other people follows directly from knowing that we are loving and lovable in our own right. Easily said, but much more difficult to experience. Where sexuality is concerned, we have all been indoctrinated with the belief that loving our own sexuality is very dubious, if not downright sinful. And when it comes to loving our bodies, sexuality is only a very small part of the problem of loving ourselves just the way we are. When did you last look in a mirror and feel totally delighted by the beautiful person you saw smiling back at you? The more likely result was a worried frown and a long list of defects.

The reasons for not loving our own bodies are complex, but if we don't love ourselves how are we ever going to believe that somebody else can possibly love us? What on earth can they see in me?

Most of us have been told so often that the way we look isn't good enough that it's hardly surprising that we have problems in delighting in our bodies. The models we are supposed to aspire to – the people in colour magazines and on television – just don't look like us. They don't have problems with their bodies like we do. At the same time we are pressured to wear clothes that inhibit our movement and to eat unhealthy food, and then to medicate ourselves against the effects of lack of exercise and good diet. No wonder it feels like a plot designed to make us feel the wrong size and shape, ugly, ill and undesirable. It feels like a plot because it *is* a plot. In order to sell us things that change our bodies, whether food, fashions or drugs, the companies that create the product have to convince us that the way we are without their products is abnormal and unnatural, a situation that can only be saved by buying them.

The way breasts hang from a woman's chest is unnatural, so let's persuade her to buy an expensive bra to hold them up. He's having problems getting an erection, so let's sell him a pornographic magazine and some 'Hot Jock' erection cream to help him do it properly. And it's no help at all that she has rarely seen other women's breasts, except the ones in magazines and travel brochures which are specially chosen to perpetuate the myth of the standard beautiful breast. He's probably never seen another erect penis, except maybe in a carefully posed porno magazine.

Everyone is fine just the way they are. While it's true that our bodies could probably benefit from eating more healthily and getting more exercise and fresh air, loving yourself exactly as you are is fundamental to enjoyable intimacy. Beware of normality – we're all different. Beware of feeling bad about your body – it's almost certainly because other people have expectations that nobody can fulfil. Beware of spending a lot of money to improve your looks – money can't buy you love.

If loving our bodies is problematic, loving our own sexuality is even more difficult. For most of us as children, finding out that we were sexual was a very secret and naughty thing. When our parents caught us touching or stroking ourselves, they usually either pointedly ignored us, or we were punished. In particular, masturbation was very embarrassing, and was either not talked about at all or was associated with the threat of terrible consequences, especially for boys. Because the signs of orgasm for girls are less obvious, it conveniently complemented the belief that nice girls don't have sexual feelings.

Most of our early memories of sexual self-exploration are connected with guilt and secrecy. Like the private things we do in the toilet, masturbation was for me a very private and secret thing. It can't have gone unnoticed, since the 'soiled' hankies disappeared from under my bed very promptly, but nobody ever mentioned it.

Sex may have been brought more into the open in recent years, but masturbation still has a very bad press. Whether stated specifically or not, most sexologists still imply that masturbation of any kind is psychologically (and therefore scientifically) a very second-rate activity compared with 'real' sex. Liberating masturbation is an important part of learning to love ourselves completely, though the belief that masturbation is 'second-rate sex', together with our early memories of secrecy and guilt will, I suspect, make complete sexual self-appreciation one of the hardest parts of open and honest relating.

Masturbation is important since it is the only way of experiencing orgasm which is guaranteed not to hurt anybody else, and by the same token guaranteed not to need anybody else's approval nor to lead to physical rejection. With such built-in safeguards it has a lot to recommend it, as long as we recognise that orgasm is not the single goal of physical self-appreciation, just as intercourse is not the inevitable goal of intimacy. The concern about orgasmic failure (which is what most so-called 'sexual problems' boil down to) follows directly from the rigid belief that all physical self-appreciation is sexual and all sexual self-appreciation is orgasm-oriented, which in turn is a result of sex being singled out as something that happens only in certain bits of our anatomy – the erogenous bits. There is a danger of feeling incomplete or that you have failed if orgasm is thwarted, but the varieties of physical self-exploration are as numerous as the varieties of interpersonal closeness.

It's clear that, for most people, stroking their own genitals can be very pleasurable. Until they're told not to touch them, most babies and young children find their genitals as fascinating as their mouths and fingers. Because genital touch is so tied up in our culture with the having of sex, or at the very least with the having of orgasms, it's very difficult to think of orgasm being associated with genital stimulation but not being an inevitable result of it. At the same time the emphasis our culture puts on specifically sexual feelings makes it difficult to relate sexual feelings to other physical feelings, or to see sexual feelings in the physical and emotional context of our whole lives. The problem of distinguishing sexual feelings from other physical feelings becomes apparent when our whole body, including the 'erogenous' bits, is involved in an activity such as swimming naked, receiving a full-body massage, or dreaming an erotic dream, especially when these activities lead to sexual arousal.

Orgasm from masturbation is an important way in which we can provide our bodies with pleasurable feelings, but it's neither the only way of feeling good physically, nor the only source of self-provided sexual pleasure. As people have become aware of the importance of being in control of their sexuality and sexual feelings, there has been a good deal of emphasis on the benefits of masturbation. It has certainly been important to add masturbation to many people's repertoire of ways of feeling good about themselves, yet at the same time it has laid a lot of stress on masturbation at the expense of other ways of providing your body with sensual pleasure. Women who have read Lonnie Barbach's *For Yourself* or men who have looked at Jack Morin's *Men Loving Themselves* would be excused for believing that the ability to have wonderful masturbatory orgasms would cure anything from chilblains to acute depression.

Masturbation is just one way of being physically intimate with your own body, just as intercourse is only one way of being intimate with somebody else. To believe in either as the be-all and end-all of sexual behaviour is to miss all the other ways of experiencing physical warmth and pleasure, and there is, as might be expected, quite a difference here between the expectations of men and women, especially where intercourse is concerned.

When Shere Hite (in *The Hite Report on Male Sexuality*) asked men whether they would like it if intercourse was sometimes replaced with other intimate activities, the majority seemed not to understand the question, and three-quarters of men always wanted a close physical encounter with a woman to include intercourse. When women were asked what they liked most about sex (in the original *Hite Report*), roughly half said something other than intercourse or orgasm, the most frequently mentioned alternatives being touching, emotional intimacy, tenderness, closeness, and the sharing of feelings. 'Closeness with another person is more important to me than orgasm.' 'Good sex for me is much more than genital.' 'Too much pressure to have orgasm makes sex goal-and-success oriented and misses the whole point.' 'The emphasis on orgasm, the separation of orgasm from sensuality, warmth and openness, is unfortunate.' 'The kissing, touching, talk and tenderness that happens when two people like and enjoy each other is much more important than orgasm.' These are just a few responses to Shere Hite's question to women about the connection between sex and orgasm.

A few men, however, are beginning to realise that the relationship between closeness and sex is one of infinite variety. One of Shere Hite's male respondents wrote 'The best sex is the caressing, stroking, soothing, embracing, holding, tonguing, nibbling, the feeling of emotional intimacy, and the whole panoply of feelings and excitement, aliveness, wonder, fascination and mystery.'

Almost nobody in Shere Hite's surveys said that orgasm and intercourse were always painful experiences for them, but the range of alternatives is constantly being widened and explored. Though the realisation is slow to dawn that variety and choice in intimate behaviour is immensely liberating, more and more people are discovering that changing patterns of closeness, while maybe feeling risky, are rich in sensual and emotional rewards.

Not only is intercourse-oriented sex a very narrow view of intimate behaviour, it also makes many other assumptions about the supposed normality of 'normal sex'. It assumes that the sexual closeness is happening between a woman and a man, which puts homosexual closeness into the realm of the less-than-normal, something we shall look at in a later chapter. It assumes that many physically disabled people can never experience sexuality 'properly', because intercourse is not within their range of potential activity. It assumes that children are not capable of sexual feelings until they have experienced a real fuck, a condescending and dangerous way of thinking.

Apart from any other consideration, the concentration on sexual intercourse explains why, at least until AIDS appeared on the scene, so much of sex education has concentrated on contraception. Surely the first line of education in controlling conception should be to show young people some of the alternatives to intercourse which are just as much fun but don't make babies. The same reasoning applies to much of the concern about AIDS and other sexually-transmitted diseases.

Intercourse-oriented sex embraces a number of other

beliefs about sexuality which are far from being substantiated by many people's experience. Bernie Zilbergeld has exposed a series of myths about men and sex in *Male Sexuality*, including the myth that sex is a performance staged by men for the benefit of women, the myth of the inevitable progression to the ultimate screw, and the myth that a man will suffer irreparable physical and psychological damage if his erect penis doesn't pass through orgasm before subsiding to its usual dimensions.

What Bernie Zilbergeld has done for men, Carmen Kerr has done for women in *Sex for Women*, showing how the myths of sexual dysfunction and sexual technique perfectly complement many women's beliefs about how they should be sexually. For example, if a woman has been taught to wait for a sexual Prince Charming, she will tend to save her precious virginity for the one man whose technique justifies its loss. By that time her experience of sexual feelings may well be so limited that she finds it difficult to respond, and so becomes labelled as 'frigid' – the dysfunction trap.

Several techniques and therapies exist which help people to look at their attitudes towards sexuality, and include exercises which help them to explore their sexual feelings and look at alternative ways of relating. Many women, for example, have benefited from pre-orgasmic groupwork, and have discovered, often for the first time, the pleasure of orgasm. Anne Hooper's book, *The Body Electric*, gives a sensitive account of this sort of therapy. Other therapeutic techniques, such as co-counselling, bioenergetics and massage, can allow people to deal with their pain and fear (and joy!) about intimacy, while at the same time acknowledging the realities of oppression and limiting assumptions about human nature. While acknowledging the benefit of anything that opens up liberating alternatives for people, however, many assumptions about sexuality die so hard that even these supposedly liberating therapies often embrace them without question.

Particularly with the growth of interest during the 1970s and 1980s in the teachings and example of the late Bhagwan Shree Rajneesh, many people became interested in the Indian techniques of tantric sex. In the West these have often become muddled with Taoist sexual traditions from China to form a body of beliefs about sexuality which centre on the concept of 'sexual energies', or, put more crudely, how to do sex properly with spiritual awareness. While many people have learned a good deal about themselves from tantra, much of the practice is very sexist. In so far as it concentrates on sexual technique and performance, it perpetuates (and in some ways seems to sanctify and legitimise) very conventional ideas about heterosexual sexuality. One such well-known manual of Eastern promise is called *Sexual Secrets*. It illustrates, among hundreds of others, a position called 'The Herd of Cows', in which a man simultaneously has his penis and both sets of fingers and toes in the vaginas of five women. The women look smug and rather bored. This must surely be the ultimate in oppressive male sexual fantasy.

Many people interested in contemporary spirituality will be aware of a widespread idea that 'male' and 'female' energies which permeate the universe are working within every human being to produce 'balanced' people. The concept has a long history, from the (fairly late in historical terms) connection between the ancient Chinese dualities of 'yin' and 'yang' with woman and man, to Carl Jung's theory of male and female archetypes.

While there is little question that we should be looking at ways of integrating the best of what have traditionally been seen as 'male' and 'female' skills and qualities, if we are not careful we can easily be lulled into believing that yin and yang are as polarised and as immutable as the sex roles of Western society. The ancient Chinese never intended their way of thinking to convey such a fixed world view, and to me these concepts of 'male/female balance' have little meaning as long as they perpetuate an unproven belief that biological (or even worse, cosmic) differences are fated to divide men and women for ever. They often seem to suggest that the double standard of sexism permeates even the most 'universal' of philosophies and cosmologies.

Sex is such a problem area for so many people that it often seems that sexuality was created especially to make our lives difficult. It would frequently be so much easier if sex didn't exist, which makes it hard to believe that joyful and painfree intimate relationships are a realistic goal. Yet I firmly believe that such a goal is realistic. While trying to understand and deal with everything that makes relating difficult, the belief that exciting and stimulating closeness can exist without pain and guilt is not only what motivates me to write about it at such length, but is also, I believe, why most people continue to relate intimately with each other despite all the problems.

Related to the problematic nature of sexual closeness is the belief that close relationships are always very complicated. People often seem to experience closeness as being relatively easy in the early stages while they are still 'in love'. But after a while reality reimposes itself, the rosy spectacles fall away, and the complexity of everything overwhelms the helpless participants. As we get to know more and more about somebody and they about us, and as the two of us spend time together, our lives should increasingly be enriched by each other's company and experience. But there is no intrinsic reason why choosing sexual closeness should necessarily complicate things. Again it means working against what we have been taught about 'not getting involved' and 'being careful', but, as with the supposed problematic nature of sexual-

ity, I cannot believe that sex is specially designed to make
life complicated.

The biggest apparent paradox of sexuality is deciding
whether or not sex is important in relating to people. The
following conversation might illustrate the point.

'Why did you do it?'

'Because it seemed the right thing to do.'

'But why did it need to be sexual? Why was it so
important to go all the way?'

'It's not important. It just followed quite naturally.'

'But if it's not important why did you have to do it?'

'I didn't have to. We chose to.'

'It seems odd that you always choose to and never
choose not to.'

'But it's important not to be limited.'

'Then it's obviously important to you that you *are*
sexual.'

'It would have been unnatural not to be sexual.'

'You just said that sex wasn't important in the way you
relate to people.'

'It's not. I can relate to people without being sexual.'

'Then why did you do it?'

Is sex important in redefining and exploring closeness
between people or isn't it? There are two ways of making
something unnecessarily important: to ignore something
that is obviously very significant to us, or to pay so much
attention to something that nobody can ignore it even
when they want to. Sex falls into both categories simultaneously.

In suppressing all mention of sexuality in much of our
lives, as we have been taught to do, sex takes on a secret
life of its own, quite separate from our everyday experience. Importance through exclusion creates sex education
as something distinct from ordinary education, makes
sexual behaviour different from everyday behaviour, and

gives us a sex life which is discussed in hushed tones separately from our real life. Sex becomes important because it is forbidden and rather daring.

According to popular history, the 1960s changed all that. Many people who grew up during that period learned to celebrate sex as the exciting and important experience it really is, with sex books, sex films, sex shops, sexual freedom, and being exhorted to make love instead of war. Sex was suddenly liberated, and the new-found freedom to describe people's sexual exploits in print and on the screen gave sex a new importance. But in highlighting sex and virtually ignoring the thousand and one other ways of getting close to people, this 'new sex' fell into the opposite trap of importance through exaggeration.

Sex needs to be brought out of its hiding place and enjoyed as one of the really good things our bodies can experience, but the clandestine importance sex has held for so long makes it very difficult to see at the same time that sex is certainly enjoyable, but is also only one pleasure among many.

With the so-called liberation of sex, sexuality was put on the open market and sold like washing powder, breakfast cereal and chocolates. If you want to make people buy your product you have to make them believe they can't manage without it, and that it will change their life, make people love them, and make them happy. As with Milk Tray so with sex – neither on its own can ever be the key to total transformation and happiness.

Physical closeness needs to be liberating for everyone, to become an essential yet not exaggerated part of their everyday experience. But it's very easy for 'liberation' to become an excuse for exactly the sort of competitive race for sexual experience that leads to people feeling left out and inadequate. This is particularly true for women, since most of the media models of physical (mostly implying sexual) closeness are created by men.

The subtle interplay of importance through exclusion and importance through exaggeration goes a long way towards explaining the seeming paradox of the conversation a couple of pages back. The explanation is that sex is, at the same time, too important to exclude from the process of getting close, and not so important as to single it out as the be-all and end-all of close encounter. It's not all that important *to* be sexual, but equally it's not all that important *not* to be sexual. Sex *is* important, but sensitive closeness is by far the most important area to explore as we learn how to get close to people in new and satisfying ways.

7

Romantic Fictions

When we were born, we became more than just a separate human being. We also became part of a family, usually consisting of mummy, daddy, the baby, and maybe an older brother or sister or two. Most of the earliest memories we have of other people are of mummy and daddy – mostly mummy, sometimes daddy, often a lump of indistinguishable mummyanddaddy.

Mummy, daddy and the children – a nuclear family, conventionally the perfect solution to how people should relate to and get everything they need from one another. The mummy and daddy are married, they love each other, they are faithful to each other (whatever that means), and everybody is very very happy.

Children and adults can of course be intensely happy together, and there's no denying that a long-term loving and supportive relationship between an adult and a growing child, the relationship that parenting offers, has enormous potential for adult and child alike. Yet at the same time the parent/child relationship is probably the most limiting of close contacts that most of us have experienced.

It's strange and rather sad to think of this relationship, which can be so exciting and liberating, as the biggest block to most people's developing freedom, but when as adults we remember who stopped us doing the adventurous things we wanted to, for most of us it was our parents.

Some of our best memories will be of our parents too; even when they were controlling us they were often protecting us from dangerous things. Whatever else, they always believed they were doing their best for us. Children are smaller than adults, and the general belief is that they can't look after themselves. Mummy and daddy will do it for you, especially if you're a little girl, because little girls are easily damaged and can't do difficult things like carrying heavy weights or lighting fires. Little boys are similarly protected from overdoses of washing-up and cleaning.

The myth says that children need looking after until they are fifteen or sixteen; that they can't think for themselves until their teens; that they shouldn't tackle dangerous things like cooking or carpentry on their own; that they're not responsible and intelligent until they leave school. The facts are that until recently childhood beyond the age of ten or eleven didn't exist; that if encouraged to be independent, young people by their mid-teens are very intelligent and mature; and that being treated as children long beyond childhood bores, angers, saddens and alienates many young adults.

The myth says that children need two and only two close and loving adults – their parents – who lavish care and attention on them, often denying their own needs. The truth is that children thrive on having a network of loving and caring contacts with adults, and that children understand and are very sensitive to adults' needs when they are reasonable and clearly stated.

The myth says that mothers mother and fathers father, and the two activities are naturally different. (It's interesting that when we say 'She mothered the child' – looked after it, maybe a bit overprotectively – it's totally different from the sexual implications of the phrase 'He fathered the child'.) The woman certainly gives birth to and has the ability to breastfeed the child, but the truth is that men and women, given the necessary skill and confidence, are equally good at caring for and loving both children and babies. Much of the 'scientific' evidence for the 'natural' mothering abilities of women stems from the 1951 research of John Bowlby. While working for the British government, he explained that the reason why many children lacked love in their early childhood was 'maternal deprivation', thus strengthening the already widely held belief that women exist primarily to mother, and providing the rationale for the speedy return of wartime women workers to the kitchen sinks 'where they belonged'.

The most pervasive myth implies that children are the property of their parents, and particularly of the father whose name they bear. It says that until your offspring leave home you can if you want control their desires and movements, expect them to do what you want them to, and impose your own values and beliefs on them even when yours differ from theirs. If you want you can ensure that your children, especially your young children, never experience anything outside your own world, and you can choose for them exactly what that world will be like. 'If you want' is a crucial phrase, and many parents don't want to unnecessarily limit their children at all. Given the current models and practice in parenting, however, it is very easy for the support/guidance balance to swing too far towards guidance, or even beyond guidance to control.

That children 'belong' to their parents is highlighted by the concept of the illegitimate ('unauthorised, improper') child. By this token a child isn't considered to be a 'real' child if it doesn't have two married parents – a biological absurdity, and a usage that is very rightly disappearing as our awareness grows of the rights of each individual child.

It is important to recognise that the myths of parenting, combined with the beliefs about sex-role training that we looked at in Chapter 4, tend to limit girls more than boys. But it would be too easy to see boys as escaping the limitations of parental and sex-role limitations while girls are trapped by them.

Perhaps the most pervasive of limitations which stays with us from childhood into adult life is overdependence. We all need support and affirmation. Especially when we're low or ill or need help we depend on other people a great deal. But support between equals is very different from wanting to be looked after more than we really need to be – the result of overprotectiveness when we were young. It affects men and women differently because we were protected in different ways and from different things, but we all have it. For women, as Collette Dowling emphasises in *The Cinderella Complex*, it means that the nasty dirty commercial world outside 'the home' is often kept from girls' experience. They are protected from this 'unfeminine' reality first by their parents, especially their father, and then are expected to find another man to take over the bill-paying, house maintenance, and dealing with the outside world.

If women feel they need to be looked after by men, men's desire to be looked after and mothered by women is much more insidious. It directly conflicts with the popular belief that men are strong and independent, and can stand on their own two feet. In fact, men in general have become so used to being serviced by their women that, if they were cast adrift in a world where they would really have to fend for themselves, the indications are that men would have a hard time. One recent study found that in married households where both adult partners

were working outside the home, the women still did
eleven times as much cooking, ten times as much washing up, eight times as much cleaning and four times as
much childcare as their husbands. The men did almost
none of the laundry. Men's dependence on women
doesn't stop at practical dependence, either. In a later
chapter we shall see how men are almost entirely dependent on women for their emotional support too.

When psychologists and psychoanalysts look at relationships they often talk about mother-complexes and
father-complexes. The subject is certainly complex, but
when the men in heterosexual couples expect continuous
mothering, and the women expect to be protected from
the big world by their men, it's little wonder that men
frequently forget that their wife is not their mother, and
women forget that their husband is not their father.

When people talk about 'their' wife or 'their' husband,
it's very easy for them to fall into the trap of thinking that
people can possess other people, that people can belong
to other people.

The parent/child link is the most biologically obvious
link between people, the closest that somebody can get to
'having' somebody else, but as we've seen, even here the
idea of the child 'belonging' to the parent can be seen in
many different ways. A lot of the problem seems to lie in
what we mean by 'my people'. At its loosest, it can
simply mean that there is a genetic connection, as with
'my mother' or 'my grandchild'. It may be debatable
whether this sort of biological link has any special significance in terms of the subsequent relationship, but it is at
least descriptive of a genetic and biological reality. Another use of the possessive pronoun in relation to people
is explanatory. If I say 'This is my friend' it probably
means that I know the person quite well, but it's as much
an explanation of why somebody else is here with me as
anything else. It doesn't usually mean that I think I own

any part of them, or that they're not free to have as many other friends as they want.

The same thing isn't true when I introduce 'my girl-friend', 'my wife', or even 'my family'. If I introduce you to a friend who is with me you might, if we are holding hands or have our arms round each other, think we have some special relationship. If I introduce them as my girlfriend or my wife, then you know we have. Or at least you think you know.

Like the closeness between child and parent, closeness between two people in a long-term committed relation-ship can be immensely stimulating and rewarding for both partners. But if the parent/child relationship is often the most limiting close contact we experience in our lives, then the partner relationship runs a close second. Why is it that a relationship that most people consider to be one of the most important things in our life should give us some of the worst problems? The answer, as usual, lies in the assumptions we make about the way people relate, assumptions that drastically limit the options open to us, and that more often than not turn out to be built on very shaky foundations.

The heart of the problem is the possessiveness which lies in that little word 'my'. While 'my mother' is a biological link and 'my friend' a descriptive one, 'my boyfriend' or 'my husband', and even more 'my girl-friend' and 'my wife', is very frequently a possessive link, a link implying the ownership of property.

I believe, and I expect that not many people will disagree with me, that everybody – woman, man or child – has the right to be proud of their individual identity. Yet the practice of possessive love constantly undermines individual identity by insisting that people define them-selves in terms of others and have their only real identity through them. In so many ways the possession of women by men, and to a much lesser extent the possession of men by women, can be seen all the time in words and everyday behaviour, from conventional ritual to offhand remarks.

Look at the way that a man puts his arm round 'his' woman, often in a very possessive way (if you don't think it's possessive, see what happens if somebody else tries to put an arm round his possession). Next time you're in a meeting, watch who puts their arms along the back of their neighbours' chairs; it's likely to be a man, especially if his neighbours are women. The physical language of men 'possessing' their environment, including the women in it, is brilliantly portrayed in the 2,000 photographs of Marianne Wex's *Let's Take Back Our Space*.

Words and ritual do the same thing. When two people get married they become 'man and wife'; not man and woman as two equals, but more like person and possession. And when they are married her father 'gives her away', and she 'takes' her husband's name and 'becomes' his for ever. As Peggy Seeger sings about marriage in her 'Talking Matrimony Blues' – 'What's yours is his, what's his is yours . . . and you're his'. The common language of sex repeats the possessive theme – he 'takes' her, robs her of her maidenhood, possesses her sweet delights.

Which brings us to romance, and the standard ways (learned from films and novels) of proving to somebody that you love them a lot:

'I never want to lose you. I'll be yours for ever.'
'Oh yes, my sweet one, my most precious, my own.'

They kiss passionately and disappear into the sunset clinging tightly to each other, never again to be torn asunder.

Nobody can ever belong to anybody else, and it's a strange idea that we can give ourselves away, or expect somebody to give themself to us. The rigid belief in possessive love is deep and pervasive, and often difficult to contradict. Yet such a belief completely denies the importance of individual choice and the clear communication of what people want – exactly those things as we saw in the last chapter that are important to happy and fulfilling intimacy. Not surprisingly, the alternatives to possessive love are as numerous as the alternatives to goal-oriented intimacy, and I shall return to them soon, but first let us look at yet another paradox of close relating: exclusiveness.

The very mention of lovers conjures up a picture of two people, eyes only for each other, forgetful of the world outside, shutting out unwanted gaze and comments. It seems so natural that people should come in pairs – the happy couple, hand in hand. Our experience tells us that there is something very special about the way two people can relate to each other that can't happen when other people are present too.

Close contact with just one other person has undeniable advantages. You can give one other person your undivided attention and they can give you theirs. It's very easy to be physically close to one other person in a way you can't in a group – three people, for example, can't easily walk along all holding hands with each other. There's always somebody in the middle with two friends, and two people on the end with only one each. The list of advantages goes on: it's obvious that frequent, open and loving one-to-one relating is vitally important in everybody's lives. Yet very often one-to-one contact involves much more than simply being with one other person and relating deeply and openly with them. We frequently feel as if we can only relate deeply and openly when we are alone with that special friend, particularly when physical closeness is involved.

The problem is not in enjoying and valuing one-to-one contact; it's to do with the emphasis that is placed on certain kinds of relating in twosomes which makes coupledom the goal of all relating. It's very like the supposed normality of goal-oriented sex which negates the equally fulfilling alternatives. Relating in couples, with all that that implies, can be an excellent way of getting close to people, but it's only one way of relating among many.

The short step from one-to-one contact to the coupledom that our society almost universally expects is all too easy to take, together with all the limitations that go with it. Coupledom is expected to start in the mid-teens, and so isn't expected of children, though girls and boys playing mummies and daddies get the idea very early on. Thereafter, coupledom is totally accepted and supported, from boyfriends and girlfriends to marriage partners, and is just as common in homosexual relationships as in heterosexual ones.

Especially when set in the mould of marriage, coupledom is expected to fulfil nearly all of our important human needs. It's certainly a very popular institution, so most people must think it's the only way to fulfil those needs. Well over 90 per cent of British people are or have been married by the time they're forty-five, and nearly every adult will have had some experience of an exclusive monogamous heterosexual relationship. In a rapidly changing world, coupledom often gives people a safe place where they can relax and be themselves. In committing themselves to be long-term friends, people becoming couples give each other the rare opportunity to get to know each other extremely well. In making a joint commitment to parenting, partners can give children a sustained closeness and support that might otherwise be very difficult. Yet safety and understanding, and even supportive and loving childcare, can be found equally well outside coupledom, and, as well as the advantages, coupledom has many drawbacks.

So far I've been using coupledom and marriage almost

interchangeably. Everything I've said about coupledom certainly applies to the state of being married, and many of the assumptions about being married follow directly from assumptions about coupledom. But because of the very powerful and precious status that has been given to marriage, it is important to look at what being married means to the people who decide to take their coupledom into marriage, and what it means in the eyes of the society and culture in which they do it.

The extension of coupledom into marriage does many things. Marriage legalises coupledom, and makes the marriage partners conform to the enormous range of legal definitions of marriage, using the supposed benefits of security and property rights to balance loss of freedom and individuality. Marriage also formalises coupledom, and gives it a neat label which everybody can understand – and relate to in the usual conventional ways. Once you're married, you have a right to expect things of your partner – sex, servicing and support, among many other things. And marriage sanctifies a certain sort of coupledom, suggesting that marriage (and by implication everything that goes with it) is divinely ordained, giving it a religious stamp of approval.

Paradoxically, many people who get married see it as an escape, a newfound freedom. If, as it has traditionally been, marriage is the main reason for leaving the parental home, then getting married becomes a proof of being grown up, a valid excuse for getting away from your parents. Yet the hope of freedom in a conventional marriage is usually a forlorn one, especially for a woman; it's all too often a move from the limitation of a child's freedom by her parents to the equally oppressive limitation of the wife's freedom by her husband.

A lot of people have a strong investment in the continued existence of marriage as the only acceptable way for people to relate intimately with one another. The barrage of justification for marriage is deafening: no wonder the small voice of rational questioning can rarely be heard. Men have an enormous interest in maintaining marriage; how else can a man keep 'his' woman under control, make sure 'his' children are looked after, ensure that 'his' home is warm and welcoming when he comes home from a hard day at work?

The parents of marriageable children also have an interest in maintaining marriage: it's what they had to do, after all, and any suggestion that there are different ways of relating invalidates all their own married hardships and struggles. Those who believe in the 'natural' link between married coupledom and children also want to maintain the institution of marriage. Where the married home is considered to be the only normal setting for happy and healthy children, any other arrangement is fervently believed to lead to inevitable suffering and deprivation. The 'broken homes' image of 'illegitimate' children is constantly purveyed to children and parents in unmarried relationships, with ample doses of blame and disapproval.

All the systems based on conventional patterns of relating depend for much of their existence on the continued existence of marriage. Our economic system couldn't exist as it is if women, married to home and children, didn't service the male workforce. Our religious system depends to a large extent on the continuation of the traditional family, with marriage at its heart, as do our legal and tax systems. It's important to remember that these systems, however monolithic they appear, consist of people, and the people who control the systems are nearly all men. It's not difficult to see the link between their personal interests and the legitimisation of those interests into supposedly 'natural' social, economic and legal structures.

Marriage thus formalises and legalises the assumptions

of coupledom, but, whether married or not, those assumptions are often the same with or without the legal licence. The children playing mummies and daddies and the teenagers on the lookout for girlfriends and boyfriends are all seen as rehearsing for the real thing: marriage. The expectations and assumptions of both rehearsal and performance are similar, the only difference is that you're allowed to make more mistakes in the rehearsal.

In the transition from one-to-one contact to conventional coupledom, the one activity that is carefully curtailed is closeness, that basic human need I have stressed so much. You may be getting closer to your partner, but you will also almost inevitably be distancing yourself from everybody else, so that people moving into coupledom often find themselves receiving less closeness rather than more.

Although it isn't often considered in the early stages of getting to know someone, the realm of exclusivity in question in coupledom and marriage is physical closeness; more specifically, sexuality. It is generally understood that as soon as you are going steady with someone, and certainly when you decide to marry them, you are not going to be sexual with anybody else. While sexuality is the activity that conventionally and legally distinguishes a faithful (good) relationship from an unfaithful (bad) one, the extension of the label 'sexual' to cover many sorts of intimacy means that most people, when choosing to be one of a couple, are also choosing not to be physically close to anybody other than their partner. And if marriage is taken as meaning 'until death us do part', the commitment can be for a very long time. Thus coupledom, and especially marriage, is a very exclusive institution; it physically excludes everybody except your partner.

But, you may say, what's wrong with men and women

falling in love with each other and marrying and having children? Why question something that seems so totally natural, something that people have always done, something that works so well?

It's very difficult to prove that there is anything at all natural about exclusive lifelong heterosexual coupledom. If exclusivity is so natural and marriage works so well, why have over 70 per cent of men and maybe half of the women in supposedly exclusive marriages felt it important to find somebody else to be physically intimate with, and why do more than a third of British and half of American marriages end in divorce? Like so many of the 'natural' elements of relating, coupledom has 'scientific' backing to prove just how natural it is. It comes from biologists, the most influential being Desmond Morris, who would like to convince us that human beings do something called pair-bonding – a sort of primeval urge to seek out and cling to one and only one other person (of the other sex) for all their physical closeness and shared sexuality. After all, without the biological mechanism of pair-bonding and the social training of coupledom, how would young people ever learn about the joys of marriage? Desmond Morris sees divorce and sexual needs outside the pair-bond arising because we haven't quite got the hang of pair-bonding yet, but he hopes that given a few more thousand years we might get the idea. We are only human.

It's certainly not true that people have always related in mummy/daddy/baby-type ways. Just because it's the usual way of relating in our society, and because we have an idea that our society is very good and advanced, we tend to ignore the alternative models that other cultures provide, and a lot of rather embarrassing historical evidence.

There are many societies in the world where marriage-like coupledom is rare or unknown, and where polyandry (one woman marrying several men), polygyny (one man marrying several women), parallel marriage (more than one marriage at a time), sexual autonomy inside and outside sanctified marriage, and marriage between two women, are perfectly legitimate alternatives. 'How typical of uncivilised primitive foreigners' I hear someone say, but I believe, together with anthropologists like Margaret Mead, Bronislaw Malinowski and Elizabeth Fisher, that we can learn a lot about the way our relationships can be from seeing how people like the Trobriand islanders of the Pacific, the San of south-west Africa, Australian aboriginals, Samoans and Eskimos traditionally conduct their physical closeness and sexual relations.

In the not-too-distant past a wide variety of relating was much more widespread than now. It's too easy to believe that the standard nuclear family is of much greater antiquity than it is. The popular picture of caveman pulling cavewoman round by the hair, or of 'early man' huddling round the campfire in neat mummy-and-daddy units, is almost certainly way off the mark. Elizabeth Fisher, in her brilliant book *Woman's Creation*, has shown that until paternity was discovered there was no basis for the recognition of a father/child relationship. Like many native Australian and Pacific cultures at the time of their first contact with Westerners, until you know about the biological technicalities of conception there is no particular reason for connecting the pleasures of sexuality with the process of pregnancy and birth. Men and women make love, and women give birth, but if both are a constant part of everybody's experience, why connect sexual intercourse and birth?

Elizabeth Fisher goes on to show that in the early neolithic cities of southern Turkey, at a time around 8,000 years ago when the art of breeding animals was still being discovered and the connection between copulation and birth was still little understood, burial arrangements suggest that the nuclear family had not yet been invented. A woman and her children were invariably buried together and the men buried separately, quite unlike most later group burials where one man, one woman and their children were buried together.

So marriage-like coupledom is far from being the universal institution which most people in our society fondly believe. But it might still be justified if the people who had chosen it as a way of relating were really happy with it. The facts suggest otherwise. Apart from the large proportion of divorces (and non-married couples tend to 'split up' just as painfully and finally as marriage partners), there is a great deal of discontent within a great many marriages. There are good things too, especially near the beginning of the relationship, but in most marriages, by the time the children reach school age, things have deteriorated. Many researchers have found that women's responses at this stage of their marriage show that general marital satisfaction is low, positive daily companionship is low, satisfaction with children is low, and negative feeling is high.

This is a tricky area of human experience to assess. Happiness is an elusive quality, feelings change all the time, and it's difficult to know how happy you are if you don't have much idea about how happy you could be if things were different. As Jessie Bernard points out in *The Future of Marriage*, human beings have an enormous capacity to adjust to almost anything, including current ideas about how people should relate and how they should marry. The question is not so much whether people can reconcile themselves to coupledom or marriage. Of course they can, and in the circumstances they can be very happy. What many people are now asking is: Are there alternatives that would be better?

Looking at the problems of relating does not negate the many happy and fulfilling times that people in couples spend together. Discontent within marriage and marriage-like relationships is not increasing because marriage is getting worse, it's increasing because people realise that they don't need to harness themselves to the abstract cause of marriage in the way that their parents and grandparents felt they had to.

Neither does looking for better alternatives negate the way we (or our parents or grandparents) have related in the past. Looking for ways in which things could be better doesn't necessarily mean that things have been bad, and even if they have been we all do the best we can within the constraints we feel bound by. There is a danger in advocating alternatives in relating in such a way that makes people feel they haven't been doing it right up until now, that they've wasted their whole life doing it wrong. Even if their marriage hasn't been all sweetness and light, to tell somebody who has been married for forty or fifty years that marriage is limiting and it would have been better if they'd done it all differently isn't going to make them feel any better.

While acknowledging people's experience and realising that nothing can change the past, it is equally important to recognise that it's never too late to change things. It's very tempting to think that once you've had children you need to maintain a relationship just as it is for them, or to believe that you're too old to make changes now.

Just like sexuality, coupledom is riddled with assumptions, very few of which are ever brought out into the open and looked at, and it's time now to look at some of them.

8

The Love Which Us Doth Bind

While attempting to fill basic human needs, coupledom sets limits on the way that the people in the couple can be together, and the ways they can be with people outside the couple. If you are choosing to spend time exclusively with somebody, you are also choosing not to spend that time on your own, or with anybody else, and the choice of how to spend our time and who with is one we are constantly having to make.

Yet we often feel we don't have any choice at all, especially when we have committed ourself to one other person. This is very much to do with the emphasis that most people place on coupledom as the best and ultimate way of relating. By this definition, being a single person is definitely a problem. On the one hand, celibacy is seen as frustrating and lonely, while relating with more than one other person is seen as highly risky, daringly promiscuous, and probably sinful.

The paradox is that while one-to-one relating has great advantages, coupledom almost always assumes several other things that one-to-one relating doesn't demand at all. Among these assumptions are:

❀ That one person is able to fulfil all of our needs to be

close, especially physically close, to another person.

❀ That love is a limited commodity, and we only have a certain amount to give and take. Therefore the more people we are intimate with, the thinner the love is spread out and the harder it is to love each person properly.

❀ That we can only have one intimate, loving and committed relationship at a time, which leads to a belief that monogamy is the only way to relate closely.

❀ That when we and our partner are together, we will be very together, sharing experiences, the same space, and the same bed.

❀ That if we make a commitment to relate to somebody for a long time, we can't change our mind later (put another way, that marriage – or a marriage-like relationship – is for life). We can't as easily decide to unmarry, and if we do, it's usually viewed as bad or unfortunate.

❀ That the specific defining factor of coupledom, indeed of all intimate relationships, is sexuality.

❀ That what we do in couples is a very private and secret thing, and is better not shared or even talked about with anybody else.

These beliefs are very widely held, but where do they come from, what function do they serve, and does people's behaviour conform to their beliefs?

The conventional marriage, and only to a slightly lesser extent the conventional couple, is built around a belief that everybody is looking for one other person – Ms or Mr Right – to complete their life and give them everything they need. Most people in couples do recognise that they need other friends in their life to share their different interests, but it's also noticeable that it can be very difficult to be close friends with somebody who is half of a couple. It's fine to work with somebody who is half of a couple, or to be with them in a group of friends, but it's not the same if you want to spend a lot of time alone together, and certainly not the same if you want to be physically close to each other.

I choose different people to do different things with at different times. One person can't fill all my needs for friendship, and I can't fulfil all of anybody else's. But I've been taught that I need more than 'just good friends'. I've been told that I need just one important person to be very close to, who will understand and support me, love me and look after me. And someone like that is very difficult to find in this cold and unfriendly world.

This sort of longing is a very common feeling, but if I put the problem this way I've already made three quite unnecessary assumptions. If I believe the world is cold and unfriendly then it's only to be expected that I shall fall into the arms of the person who gives me real attention, warmth and openness. If I believe that it's very difficult to get close to people, the first person to achieve that seemingly impossible feat will be the answer to my dreams. And if, as I've always been told, and romantic novels and films confirm, I believe that I can only have one very deep and meaningful relationship, I'm instantly ruling out the possibility of having two or more deep and meaningful relationships in my life.

Nearly everybody has a deep fear of being alone and abandoned in a cold and hostile world. Like many fears, it comes largely from a lack of closeness and attention all through our lives, especially when we were young. The feelings of separation and loneliness aren't helped by the abruptness with which we were separated from our mothers when we were born, ending the only nine months of total care and attention we have ever known. It's a fear that is provoked and exaggerated in many ways, from emphasising the problems of being single to the rigged violence and suspense of horror films. It's no coincidence that the latest crop of terror from the film-makers plays largely on the fear of being alone in a big house with horrible unknown violent things happening around a terrified inmate.

No wonder we run into the arms of the nearest friendly person and cling tight. Unfortunately this ties in directly with our belief in the one and only one close relationship. Clinging tight to somebody is physical and therefore meaningful, and it's an easy step to believing that this is *the* person. In order to be supportive and give you the attention you need, this friendly person needs to be warm and open, and that too seems a very rare attribute. So this must be for real. This must be love.

To hear many people talk about love you would imagine it being like money or water – something that you have in a fixed quantity and give away as you think fit. Once you've given it away you don't have it any more, and the more people you give it to the less you'll be able to give to each person.

'Do you love me?'
'Of course I do.'
'Then what's going on with Leslie?'
'Well, I love Leslie too.'
'How can you love Leslie when you say you love me?'

How indeed? There is so often the feeling that if a close friend of yours is being close to someone else, they're taking something away from you. That's because they *are* taking something away from you, but it's almost certainly not their love. What they are taking away is their physical presence, and in the process removing their immediate attention from you.

What you choose when you choose to be with different people at different times is not how much you love each of them, but very simply how much time you spend with each of them, how much attention you give them while you're with them, and what you do with them – and these will vary every time you are with someone. There's no reason at all why you need to stop loving someone because you're not with them, and no reason why you have to not love somebody that you're with because you're already loving somebody else. If you can't be with the one you love, love the one you're with.

In very practical terms the amount of time you want to spend with another person is probably the most critical decision in any relationship, far outweighing the nebulous task of trying to quantify the amount of love each person is feeling, and transcending any particular label attached to the relationship.

As I said earlier, if you are choosing to spend time exclusively with somebody, you're choosing not to spend it alone or with anybody else. This is fine, as long as you are aware of the implications of your choice. You can't be alone with two different people at the same time, so you have to keep choosing who to spend your time with. It changes all the time: just at the moment my priority is being on my own, later it might be spending time with one of my children, tomorrow other people will share time with me.

This constant choice is as true of a thirty-year-old marriage as it is when you first decide to spend time with somebody, and it's too easy to think that once you've made the decision in relation to somebody else, it will always be like that. It won't, and I know many people who made the marriage vow to be mutual help and company yet hardly ever see each other, spending far more time with other people than with their partner. This is not necessarily a bad thing, as long as the amount of time they are spending together is a mutually agreed choice. If it isn't a conscious choice, it leaves the stage wide open for the well-known bogeys of rejection, isolation and jealousy.

Falling in love implies a mutual attraction and a recip- rocation of attention, and, although it is often true, it's usually tacitly assumed that both participants will want to spend a great deal of time with each other. But what if one wants to spend more time with the other than the other wants to spend with the one? I suspect that this is nearly always the case in any relationship, and although the balance of wanting time together will vary from friend to friend and from time to time, it is a particularly difficult problem if you are choosing to relate closely only to one other person. The feelings that this situation can often arouse are of unfairness and rejection, and if you have chosen exclusive monogamy as a way of relating, to be the loser in the time equation can be very painful.

The commonest (though I think the least aware) way of dealing with a situation like this is that one person gives in to the way the other wants it to be. The alternative solutions depend on the participants being as clear as they can about how much time they do want to spend together – usually they will be able to come to some compromise. If what one person offers simply isn't acceptable to the other, however, then they might well choose not to continue the closeness. I know this sounds a bit cold and clinical, but I would much rather be clear about what I and the other person want from our time together, which can be talked about in a very caring and supportive way, than suffer the agonies of feeling rejected and left out when our togetherness stops too soon for me, or the pain of wanting someone to go away and being too frightened to say what I want.

Another of the official religious reasons for marriage is as a remedy for sin and adultery, which upholds the common belief that you can only have one special, close, intimate and important relationship at a time. The argu- ment seems a bit circular to me, like the notice in the park that says 'It is forbidden to throw stones at this notice'. If marriage didn't exist, neither would adultery, so why create marriage to deal with a problem that wouldn't arise if marriage didn't exist?

Monogamy – 'marrying' only one person at a time – follows directly from the twin beliefs of one person being able to fulfil all your needs and love being a limited commodity. If you have one special person to provide everything you need in a relationship, and if you only have a limited amount of love, then obviously all your love must go on that one special person.

I tend to agree with Elizabeth Fisher's historical analysis of the roots of monogamous marriage, which ties in with the possessiveness of many relationships. As we saw in Chapter 7, the discovery of paternity added women and children to the list of potential things a man could own to give him status. Without paternity there is nothing to show that men have any part in making children; with the knowledge of paternity the only concrete link that men have with their children, and therefore with the future (including the future of their amassed possessions), is the mother of the child. It therefore becomes very important to possess the mother so you can keep track of your offspring, and it also becomes important to control the fertility of your woman so that you know for certain that the children she is bearing are yours. Limiting your ownership of women to one at a time makes it easier to keep a check on her, and ensures that there are enough women to go round all the men that want one.

I am aware that this is a tentative and simplistic way of looking at the development of a complex institution, but it is true that in the way that monogamous marriage is currently organised the elements of the analysis do hold, and in general it is men who stand to get much more out of marriage than women. There is a general assumption that husbands do in many respects own their wives. The assumption is typified by legal and fiscal rules about husbands being responsible for (having a right to in many cases) their wife's earnings, women taking their husband's name on marrying, and housework and other services done for husbands not being real work and therefore not paid for. It can be traced through men's attitudes towards the sexual experiences of their wives, like the man who checks every time his wife goes away alone to see that she's left her diaphragm at home, and the similar ways in which men will react to protect their property and their wives from intrusive male competition.

The logical extension of one person being able to fulfil all your needs is that once you've found the person, you need never be apart:

'I'll be yours for ever.'
'Yes, darling. We'll never be separated. We'll always be together.'
And off they go to share every experience, set up house together, sleep in the same bed. Very together, for ever.

When we hear about somebody else's experiences or tell them about our own, we learn a lot about the world and how other people see it, but if we try to have the same experiences as somebody else it's very easy to end up living through them. This is a particular danger for women since the romantic ideal is to lose yourself to your man, stop being yourself at all and become the doctor's wife or the pop star's girlfriend. In some ways it is very convenient to live through somebody else's experience, since you don't have to take so many risks, but the loss of your own identity is far too large a price to pay for getting close to someone. In the final analysis we can only have our own experience, nobody else can have it for us, and we can't give experience to them.

Setting up house together is another potential pitfall of

overtogetherness. It is very easy to overlook the need that every human being has for privacy and the freedom to choose not to be with the person or people we live with, however much we love them. As well as choosing how to spend our time (and choosing who to be with, including ourself), everybody ideally needs – as Virginia Woolf clearly pointed out in a 1929 essay – a room of their own, especially women, who have traditionally been denied it. It's also important to know who is going to look after any joint living space that you create with someone, because, even with the best will in the world, unless you consciously choose to do it differently, there's a great danger that the woman in a heterosexual couple will end up doing nearly all the housework whether she chooses to or not.

The main problem for many people, especially once they have become half of a couple, is in finding the physical space that they need. Houses are designed around the concept of verytogetherness. The one lounge, the one dining room, the one kitchen, and the one largish 'master' bedroom, are all designed for multiple occupancy. If there is one room designated as a study, it's too easy to assume it will be his. The problem is compounded by each room being designed for a very specific purpose, and 'spare' rooms as opposed to 'main' rooms being in general far too small to be comfortably alone in for any length of time.

So on to the double bed, that universal symbol of coupled bliss, yet a very confused symbol. When you get very close to somebody, one of the things you may choose to do is sleep together, whatever you mean by that ambiguous phrase. Whether or not it includes a sexual dimension – and it's important to remember that it never has to – sleeping in the same bed as somebody you like very much is usually extremely pleasant, even if you sometimes don't get very much sleep. When you become a couple, the expectation is that you will both sleep in the same bed all the time, or at least when you're in the same place. It's a proof of togetherness, and for most people a proof of sexual involvement. If it's discovered that a couple aren't sleeping in the same bed, it must be a sign that things between them aren't as they should be, that they've lost interest in each other.

I have no figures to prove it, but I would guess that people in long-term couples, most of whom are married, spend many more nights in their double beds not being sexual than nights that include shared sexuality. I also expect that nights spent together that include shared sexuality, or even cuddling, become less common in most relationships as time goes on.

If the people in a couple don't want to be particularly close in bed every single night of their lives, why do they continue to do it? The answer is that most people have never considered the possibility of an alternative. Double beds and marriage go together like a pair of chopsticks. That's why housebuilders, furnishers and hotel operators assume that one big bedroom with one big bed will almost universally accommodate two people. The practicalities of not sleeping together in the average modern house or flat involve twin beds in the same room (which doesn't improve privacy), or one person being relegated to the single bed in the spare room.

Another reason for never sleeping apart is that it's very easy to get addicted to sleeping together. The language is indicative of a drug-like dependency – 'I can't sleep without you being there'; 'I need you to be with me'; 'I'm scared if you're not there'.

In a relationship where shared sexuality is assumed to be important, yet the partners don't talk about it much as time goes on, the double bed and what sometimes happens in it become the main proof of a continuing sexual involvement. And it's not only proof for the people in the couple – 'If he sleeps with me, he must still love me and think I'm attractive' – it's also proof for other people. Thus if they are sleeping together all is well, and if they're not sleeping together there must be a problem.

Well, if two people I know are sleeping together it certainly indicates that things are conventionally as they should be, but it's a bit disappointing for me if I've ever had the idea that it would be rather nice for one of them to sleep with me one day. And it can be a bit of a problem if I go and stay with them. I may love one or both of them very much, but if they're both there it's easy for me to feel outnumbered and not get close to either of them. When I go to my lonely bed and they to their cosy double bed, it's easy for me to feel left out.

The confusion is compounded if I go to stay with a close friend who is half of a couple, and the other half is away. After all, they do have this double bed, and it's only being half used. I'm going to feel very cold and lonely in my own bed in my own room, and it seems a bit sad that the talk and closeness we've been enjoying has to stop at bedtime. But that's the way it is. I don't dare to broach the subject because I'm afraid of being rejected and, even if the thought had crossed my friend's mind, we're probably both too scared of the reactions of the absent half of the couple to risk anything.

The double bed means much more than proving to-getherness and sexual involvement between two people; it effectively excludes the physical closeness of one of those people with anybody else. The exclusive double bed has become the symbol of an exclusive couple, and the one part of a couple's territory which is out-of-bounds to anybody else. It also encourages the possessive element in coupledom – if my partner is here in bed with me then I know for certain that nobody else can get at them. It's a bit like sleeping with your purse under your pillow.

Desmond Morris's theory of pair-bonding, when

combined with the belief that one person can fulfil all our needs, results in a further assumption. This is that once we have found *the* person, we'll be with them exclusively until one of us dies. This let-out by death has for a long time been the only way that church and society have allowed the possibility of one person being physically close, usually meaning sexual, with more than one other person in their lifetime, though it seems very sad that the only way for many people to get close to somebody other than their partner is for that partner to die first.

One development of the last couple of hundred years is that while life-long exclusivity has remained a fairly static ideal, the length of people's lives has dramatically increased, so that once you do get married, you can expect to be married for longer than ever before. While this elongates the positive experiences of marriage, it also means that the limiting aspects have a chance to become very oppressive. In particular it means that, since women tend to live longer than men and are often expected to live very much through the experience of their partner, the death of their husband after a very long verytogetherness can leave a woman with little sense of self-identity and self-worth with which to start making connections with new people or strengthening links with the people the marriage has excluded.

The abrupt ending of life-long exclusive coupledom with the death of one of the partners is mirrored in the progress that most intimate relationships are expected to take, even when they don't last for long. So many sexual encounters end with a complete severance of contact that it seems the only way to do it. We get close to someone, it becomes sexual, it reaches a point where we (or they) don't want to carry on, and we split up. There's a no-more-to-be-said finality in that 'splitting up', yet this is the commonest way of describing the end of a close relationship. It's sad that it seems so difficult to choose to be good but non-sexual friends once you've been sexual with somebody, that lovers aren't allowed to be friends when they're not lovers any more.

I've already suggested that possessiveness in relating often comes from a fear of 'losing' someone. The same fear of loneliness and rejection, especially when contrasted with the good feelings of having been very close to somebody, makes it difficult to accept anything less than the closeness you have already had with them. If you can't be as close as you were last time, something is wrong. Terri Schultz, in her book *Bittersweet*, describes a special male friend who talked her into bed, and when she refused to sleep with him again he stopped seeing her. This ties in directly with the standard sexual progression, where you expect to do a bit more every time you meet somebody until eventually you reach the goal. The only conventional choices you then have are to keep proving the closeness by being sexual every time you're together, or splitting up and starting all over again with someone else. It doesn't have to be like this at all; the two of you can choose to relate in whatever way you want whenever you want, but the pervasive models of long-term sexual involvement and abrupt endings are difficult to replace.

We've come full circle back to the sexual definition of relationships, and how at the same time as keeping sexuality in the dark we centre all our current descriptions of adult relating around the belief that sexuality is their main feature. At the heart of the exclusivity of exclusive coupledom lies sexuality. As well as being what defines whether somebody is being 'faithful' to you or not, sexuality is probably the most difficult area for any couple to think about sharing outside their coupledom.

Introducing somebody as your wife or husband is at the same time reassuring, and for many people a little scary. It's so heavy with implications about possessiveness, dependence and exclusivity that I tend to wince every time somebody does it. It's a fact – they are married, therefore he is her husband and she is his wife. 'The wife', many men say, dropping the possessive pronoun to distance himself from her, but retaining the descriptive noun which only makes sense in relation to him as a man and her husband.

Though I'm talking about marriage, the same assumptions, particularly as they relate to sexuality, apply equally whatever labels the parties in a couple use to describe their relationship. Whatever the arrangements you have with a good friend for being physically close, the words you use to describe your closeness will, unless you go into great detail, invariably be taken as meaning the exclusive sexual relationship that most people expect. This makes it very difficult to describe somebody who is a special and intimate friend, but not a monogamous partner. By not having the words to describe any other sort of relationship, and by casting unwholesome suspicion on any such practice, even the possibility of the existence of more than one intimate friend is denied us. This is particularly true if you are married, when the only other sort of close physical relationship that convention allows is an affair with a mistress (where is the male equivalent?) or lover, which automatically carries the implications of secrecy and infidelity, sexual achievement, and the threat of the punishment that follows the breaking of the seventh commandment.

When Shere Hite asked the men in her survey who had been married over a year if they had had a sexual relationship other than with their wife, 72 per cent said they had. This fact alone may not surprise you, since although affairs certainly contradict the biblical strictures against adultery, many people consider that in order to keep marriage going, especially from a man's point of view, extra-marital affairs are a necessary safety-valve for suppressed sexuality. One of the things understood to define an affair is the successful achievement of the ultimate sexual goal. Usually only fully-fledged intercourse is recognised as legal grounds for there being a real problem (though the courts, with their blinkered vision, can normally only see physical closeness in terms of intercourse – try telling the judge that you were in bed naked together but didn't make love).

But sexuality is not the only necessary feature of an affair; the other is secrecy. Of all those men who had 'committed adultery', only 3 per cent thought it was important enough to their marriage to tell their partner. Some 19 per cent had been found out by their wives, and the remaining 78 per cent – 56 per cent of all married men – said they thought their wives didn't know. Thus there's a more than even chance, if you're an American woman who has been married more than a year, that your husband has been sexual with somebody else and thinks you'll never find out about it.

If you thought this was a purely American phenomenon, recent British research by Annette Lawson (described in her book *Adultery*) shows that nearly three-quarters of the married people asked had had an affair. Interestingly but perhaps not surprisingly, women were much more likely than men (47 per cent against 34 per cent) to have had a single flingette, while men were much more likely (40 per cent to 26 per cent) to have had more than four extra-marital liaisons.

Not telling the person you're closest to about an experience you've had is understandable if the experience is fairly trivial. But shared sexuality is not only very important to everybody (whether it always needs to be is another question), it's the basis on which relationships in our society are built, so you can hardly argue that you didn't think it was important enough to mention. You could say that it's part of the game of affairs not to tell, but that's hardly the open and honest communication necessary to the best relating. You might say you'd rather not know, and that when your partner isn't with you it's up to them what they do. They must choose how to live their own life, but another close relationship is bound to be important to them, and it can hardly fail to affect the way they relate to you. And if not wanting to know comes from your desire not to be hurt, the hurt that comes from dishonesty and suspicion is at least as painful as the hurt that comes from openly shared facts and feelings.

Most people (meaning mostly men in this case) don't tell their partner about their sexual activities with other people, or even their sexual feelings about other people, because they're frightened – frightened of the other person's anger, frightened of losing them, frightened that they might do the same, frightened of being rejected. The fear of telling increases as time goes on, and is fed by the practice of secrecy, so it gets harder and harder to be honest. It's much easier to tell your partner that you've met somebody very attractive who you want to spend more time with than it is to say you've had a sexual relationship with someone for the last ten years.

If fear is the main motive for secrecy, what secrecy thrives on is the assumption that personal privacy is vitally important, even when other people suffer as a result. There is a widely held belief that what happens in your personal life, especially if you're a man, is your own concern and doesn't involve anybody else. This is particularly true of your 'sex life' – heaven forbid that anybody should know the intimate details of that.

Privacy is a very two-edged concept. On the one hand it gives people the space apart from others that everybody needs – their room of their own. In this sense I would always defend anybody's right to privacy. Yet when privacy engulfs other people within the possessive grasp of the person wanting to be private, some very contradictory things happen, because the private life of the couple is a very different thing from the private life of the individual. The principle of privacy often goes too far, as when it allows old people to die alone, not to be discovered for days, or lets lonely and desperately sad people feel so isolated that killing themselves seems the only way out.

Privacy certainly goes too far where coupledom is concerned. Because the barriers between the couple and everybody else are so strong, few people would consider interrupting the couple's privacy, even when something is obviously very wrong. 'She was punched in the side of her face, dragged screaming to the ground by her hair and pulled along the street, while passers-by and four men in a nearby garage stood and watched,' reads a report in today's paper, 'because they thought the man was her husband.'

The privacy of the couple, and by extension the privacy of the family, denies individual freedom by hiding the pain and oppression of unequal relationship, and tacitly condoning anything, however hurtful and violent, that one person within that privacy does to the other. Though women and men both suffer within the walls of their coupledom, it is nearly always the woman who suffers both physical violence and mental and emotional isolation the more acutely. A quarter of all reported violent crime is wife assault, and the highest rates of depression and phobia are found among married women.

If the partners in a couple have an equal relationship there is little need for privacy, since there is nothing to hide from the outside world. It's not that the world needs to know every detail about their closeness, nor that they won't want to be alone together some of the time, just that neither of them has any terrible secrets about the relationship, and neither feels forced into a closeness they don't want.

Being trapped in marriage, and especially being the victim of physical and emotional violence within the privacy of coupledom, is the ultimate paradox of a way of relating which promises so much, yet often offers so little. Michèle Barrett and Mary McIntosh, in their book *The Anti-Social Family*, show clearly the similarities between prison and family life: '5.45 pm in a block of council flats. In each of fifty boxes a woman is frying the children's fish fingers, bathing the baby, putting its nappies in the washing machine and peeling the potatoes for the husband's tea. All the same, but in isolation'.

The dividing line between privacy and isolation is a fine one. The distinction comes from the ability to choose. Being alone, finding your own private space, is something you can choose (if you have the support and freedom to make that choice). When you are isolated the choice is taken away, and circumstances (housework, children, lack of money) close the alternative options, leaving you feeling totally powerless.

If coupledom and marriage are such big problem areas for so many people, why do we so blindly go into it? Can't we choose to do something different? The apparent paradoxes of powerlessness and choice are the next area to explore.

9

The Freedom to Choose

There's no denying that everybody needs love, closeness, warmth and support in order to live a fulfilled and satisfying life. There is also little doubt that at present most adults expect to receive the bulk of these things from the one other person in their couple. In many partnerships this arrangement works reasonably well. In many others, however, it isn't working at all, and where it isn't working there is a real need to provide alternative support systems. It's also important to be aware that even when relating is reasonably good, there is nearly always room for improvement. Though we may feel happy with things as they are, who knows without exploring the options available how much better things might be?

With accepted ways of relating defined so narrowly, one of the commonest feelings that we have in our relationships is of being trapped and tied down. It feels as though everybody and everything is forcing us to be a particular way and to play a particular role. We feel powerless to change anything, as though we have absolutely no choice other than to carry on in the same way day after day.

Yet at the same time as feeling powerless, there is

something very safe and predictable about a situation that we have grown used to. Even though we might feel trapped and tied down, we feel that it would be much harder to change things than to accept the situation the way it is. In very subtle ways we become addicted to our circumstances – trapped yet safe, limited yet predictable. We give our power away, and are supposedly content to be told what to do and how to be.

What we lose if we give up our power and become addicted to one particular way of relating is our freedom to choose our future. It can be hard to ensure that what we do is what we choose to do, rather than what we are told to do. Much of the time the pressures to conform are far from subtle, and it isn't easy to distinguish between what we want to do and what somebody else wants us to do.

It's easy enough to say it, I know, but where decisions affect your life, the most important opinion to take into account is your own. Being sensitive to the opinions and feelings of your partner, your household, your parents or your children is certainly important too, but it's *your* life, not theirs. If you are to have any chance of creating a situation that provides for your real needs, in the end any important decisions affecting it must be yours.

In order to choose and make decisions about your life, you have to know that you have some power to influence your own future. In a society where so many people have so many reasons for keeping other people powerless from infancy onwards, it's often extremely difficult to remember that you almost always have choices about how to live your own life, whatever pressures there may be to live it the way that other people want.

I'm very aware that the question of choice is a contentious issue. There are always limits to the choices available to us, and those limits vary according to our situation and resources. If I'm on supplementary benefit then I don't usually have the choice of buying a new car; if I'm black and live in South Africa I can't choose where to live; if I leave school at sixteen I can't usually choose to be a surgeon or a lecturer. Where relating is concerned, the results of not having a real choice are all too apparent. The unmarried pregnant woman is told that she'll have to get married; the woman with children who wants to work is told that her children must take priority. The man who lets his family life seep into the office or factory is told that he can't let his personal problems interfere with his work; the man seen holding another man's hand is forced to resign.

So choice is limited. But it's very easy to believe, especially when we are being told so all the time, that because choice is limited we have no choice at all. The truth is that everybody has choice – usually a wide range of choices – but it is often difficult to handle the results of choosing something other than what may appear to be the only option. Yet the injustice we do ourselves if we choose, every time, to do what we are told rather than doing what we really want is usually far more painful in the long run. The results of our taking our life into our own hands will undoubtedly upset the people who feel they have a right to tell us how to be. We cannot afford to ignore their feelings and reactions, but when those people are being critical and aggressive, it's very easy to forget that the only person who knows what is best for me is me, and the only person who knows what is best for you is you.

Taking power away from people has been a favourite game for centuries. A pecking order in society has become so commonplace that we mostly accept it as a basic component of human behaviour. Thus it becomes very difficult to acknowledge the individual importance and power of one person, especially if that person is female, black, poor, working class, disabled or homosexual.

The power to control your life, especially in the face of rampant oppression, is often a difficult thing to imagine, but it helps if you can begin to see what and who it is that has an investment in keeping you powerless.

When I'm talking about power, I need to make an important distinction between power in the sense of 'power over', which is the way that the word is so often used in contemporary politics, and power in the sense of 'individual powerfulness'. There is an interesting parallel here to the last chapter's thoughts about privacy. As long as power is seen in terms of a person's strengths and abilities, it is obviously an important and positive quality. When that power reaches out to control other people, denying them their own power, it turns into a very manipulative and devious thing, limiting other people's freedom and forcing them to do things they don't want to do.

Many people are powerless because their power has been taken away quite wilfully. Governments take power away from minorities; the police take power away from suspects; schools take power away from children. Men take power away from women in a great variety of ways – denying them money, refusing to share housework and childcare, physically and mentally violating them and their needs. But for all the power that is taken away from people quite deliberately, disempowering people is often a much more subtle process, and those taking away the power can often genuinely believe that it is being done for the loser's own good. This is particularly true of children, where adults automatically assume that they know what is best for 'their' children, failing to see the vital difference between support and control.

It's also common to take power away from people who can be classified as physically, emotionally or mentally ill (sometimes you have to classify them as ill precisely so you can take away their power). Again the assumption is that somebody else knows what they need better than they do themselves.

Quite often the power is taken away from the individual and given to a particular convention, and this is certainly the case in relating. It is frequently assumed that the institution of the family, or of parenting, or of marriage, is more important than the people within the institution. Until recently, marriage counselling almost invariably assumed that its function was to keep the marriage intact, rather than to find a solution that suited the individual partners which might include the ending of the marriage. 'We have to stay together for the children' is a common argument against taking individual needs into account. It seems that almost anything takes priority over the individual needs of the individual person, especially if that person is a woman.

The same is true of work. If a man's personal life is interfering with his work, it's generally assumed that his work will naturally take precedence. Money talks, after all, so if you're a man entertaining your boss to supper and your child wakes up with a nightmare during the main course, your boss is obviously the most important person to take into account.

If you're a woman it's usually rather different. You will be expected to be a good mother to your children (you can deal with the frightened child), yet you will also be expected not to let your parenting interrupt your work. This is a common double bind that leaves many women exhausted and resentful, especially since women's work, largely part-time work that allows for some flexibility in childcare, is usually so badly paid.

If the institutions of family and work keep power out of the hands of people, the would-be caring and serving institutions of national welfare do it just as effectively. The health service is supposed to be there to keep everyone healthy, but have you noticed how most doctors and specialists carefully keep their methods of healing close to their chests like some sort of magic art? They're the experts: you couldn't possibly be expected to know anything about your own health. So you go to the surgery and, before you've had a chance to explain the details of your symptoms, they've covered a prescription form with hieroglyphics and rung for the next patient.

The tax system is the same. It's supposed to be there for you and me, to ensure that everybody is provided with the basic services they need for their well-being. Woe betide you, however, if you don't fit into their neat conventional little categories – when it comes down to it, their categories are infinitely more important than your wellbeing.

And so it goes on – other people telling me what's best for me, even though most of the time I don't want them to. And what's even worse, like most of us most of the time, I believe them when they tell me what's good for me. Because people have been telling me for so long that they know what's best for me, I can very easily forget that actually *I* know best what I want. That doesn't mean not listening to them. If I've chosen to see a doctor or a solicitor, I'd be pretty stupid not to listen to them. But I can choose whether I take their advice or not. Most of the time I know roughly what the right answers are anyway: what I need is support for my decisions and help with ways of achieving what I want to do.

The giving away of power comes so easily that we often do it without noticing. After all, we have been doing it since as tiny children we gave so much of our power away to our parents and teachers. Giving power away means that we stop believing in ourselves, which is the biggest step towards letting other people run our lives and feeling trapped in a life that we didn't choose.

The seemingly impossible thing to do when you're feeling trapped is to take control of your life and change things, especially if it means taking risks and upsetting people. Yet the people who want to keep things the way they are expect you to stay powerless and do nothing, so it comes as quite a shock to them when people take back their power.

The woman in Jill Miller's novel *Happy as a Dead Cat* has five children, three pets, a husband who sits by the fire and complains if it goes out, and a father-in-law who says things like 'Shall we do the dishes for these women?' When at the end of the story she takes the children to live apart from her husband and set up a business with a friend, she certainly shocks the men, and she ends up with at least some of the advantages, leaving the men looking as happy as dead cats. As Fay Weldon says on the back of Jill Miller's book, 'How brave we are! Well, have to be . . .'

As well as the knowledge that you have control over your own life (even when it feels as though you haven't), if you are to choose what you want for yourself you have to know what options are available to you. It's here that information about alternatives is extremely important. To my mind, information sharing is what social services should mostly be about.

In most situations where a decision needs to be made there is usually a wide range of courses of action. You need to know all the relevant choices available to you, and their relative advantages and drawbacks in your particular situation. When you have the information, you are in a position to make a rational and informed choice about your own future. This has been a growing realisation in the last ten years or so, with a welcome growth in the number and variety of information services available.

Yet those people and institutions that benefit from your powerlessness also benefit from withholding information that might help you to take back your power. Thus the medical system won't always tell you if they think you've got cancer, the tax system won't tell you what information they have about you. Employers won't tell you why they are ignoring Equal Pay and Sex Discrimination Acts and paying you less than they should. Food manufacturers don't want you to know the health hazards of eating their products, and the Ministry of Defence doesn't want you to know the facts about nuclear weapons. Men don't want their wives to know the real amount of their incomes, and the police don't want you to see any records they might have on you.

These examples are all fairly specific choices that are taken away from people, thus rendering them powerless and making them feel stupid and insignificant. But there are also alternatives that don't normally present themselves because the whole structure of convention and orthodoxy is against them. It's very difficult to embark on a radical alternative to coupledom when everybody is telling you that it won't work, and it's hard to think about parenting outside a conventional family setting when nobody else you know is doing it.

This is where the supply of information within networks of similarly minded people is so important, providing support and encouragement for people who are setting out to experiment with fairly radical alternatives. We shall come back to many of these alternatives in the next chapter, but for now I'll just say that what often happens when you look at alternatives to conventional institutions and structures, whether it be communal living or natural childbirth, self-sufficiency or radical education, you'll almost inevitably find yourself connecting with a far-reaching network of people who are doing similar things, all of whom recognise the importance of information sharing and mutual support.

As soon as you have the information about possible alternatives, it becomes easier and easier to see which options might work for you and which might not. It may be that you'll choose to do exactly what you're already doing, but it will be with the advantage of knowing that there were other options, but you chose not to follow them. Knowledge about the range of alternatives sometimes seems overwhelming – it's much easier to choose between two options than between twenty – but in general the wider you cast your net for alternative strategies, the more likely you will be to find what you want.

It's often difficult, especially if you're a woman (who has probably been taught that everybody's needs come before her own), to *know* what you want. This arises because women frequently have little chance to fulfil their own needs, and little space to choose how to spend their time and use their energy. As we have seen, men are led to believe that mummy will always be there to look after them, and children are deliberately kept helpless until long after they can largely manage for themselves. All this neediness is placed firmly on the shoulders of the housewife and mother.

Being run by other people's needs is so traditionally a mother's role that when a woman asks herself what she really wants, there often seems to be nobody there to do the wanting. When she does have a rare flash of something important she wants for herself, a common reaction is to feel guilty for being selfish.

This is one of those cases (we'll look at some more later) where things are so unequal at present between men and women that it's very important every so often for women to do something that should rarely be advocated for men – to experience being totally and utterly selfish. If the men in her life can provide practical support while a woman does exactly what she wants to for a change, so much the better; if not, the world won't end simply because a woman withdraws her dependability for a day or two.

Acknowledging the importance and independence of

each person means recognising, at least in relating and probably in a good deal else as well, that there is no such thing as absolute truth. Jessie Bernard, in *The Future of Marriage*, clearly shows that in any marriage there are in fact two quite different marriages – the woman's marriage and the man's marriage. The same is true of any relationship – just because I see my relationship with you in a particular way it certainly doesn't mean that you will see it in the same way, and everybody who knows us will have their own unique way of seeing our relationship too.

There are two direct and important repercussions of this recognition. The first is that if there is no absolute reality about the relationship, there is no point in trying to force the other person to accept our version of the truth. We can certainly expect them to listen to us and support us, but as soon as we tell somebody that their version of reality is wrong and ours is right, we are doomed to non-co-operation.

The second implication of truth being in the eye of the beholder is that it is very dangerous to accept the story that one half of a partnership tells about the other half. If I meet you at a party and we are quite attracted to each other, it's one thing for me to describe the relationships in my life. But if I then start telling you that my partner is very understanding and doesn't mind at all if I have other relationships, this is the time to be wary. Not only is this my truth about my relationship with my partner; it is almost invariably angled with the purpose of validating my actions. My version of her reality can only be second-hand, and since I have a particular interest in not letting it get in the way of my relationship with you, my story is highly suspect. It doesn't necessarily stop you getting close to me, but you need to remember that my truth is only one truth.

This doesn't mean, however, that general patterns in relating don't exist independently of the partners' beliefs about the relationship. It's very easy to gloss over inequality or oppression in a relationship, and tell the person who is losing out that the problem only exists in their reality. It should be blatantly obvious by now that there are enormous inequalities in the way people live, and that oppression is so rampant that powerlessness is considered by most people to be a basic fact of human existence.

Just because a person's belief about the way things are is unique to them, it doesn't make it any the less important, and supporting people in their own unique beliefs, even when we don't agree with or understand them, is very important. If somebody believes that every man who gets close to them is going to hit them, it's not much use you telling them they're wrong, even though from your perspective you can't understand what they're talking about. At some point they will need to look at where that belief comes from, and discover any inconsistencies in their reasoning and practice for themself. Beliefs like this always have a rationale based on personal experience, and our attention and support during this process of self-discovery will be much more valuable than our criticism or advice. This doesn't mean that advice doesn't have a part to play, but it does mean that advice need only be given when it is asked for, and that the role of advice is usually to open up possibilities rather than to find the one best course of action.

Everybody's version of reality is different, and it follows that everybody's choices and solutions will also be different. Two people faced with similar problems may well handle them in totally different ways, and both, in the light of their particular considerations and beliefs, may well be right. This extends to advice, where several people giving advice might say what they would do in a particular situation, all of which could be different from what the person being advised might do. Looking at it from their own points of view, every one of those people may be right. Not only does the picture vary from one person to another, one person's situation varies from one time to another: you might solve a problem in one way today and in quite a different way tomorrow.

All of this makes comparisons of behaviour very dangerous, especially if the comparison includes a judgement of whether somebody has behaved well or badly, rightly or wrongly. Judging someone else's behaviour and actions implies that you know their version of reality at least as well as they do, a belief that they will rarely appreciate or find very helpful. For the same reason it's treacherous to compare the behaviour of two people in similar situations, especially the ways in which those two people relate to you. There are few more distressing things to hear than that a friend of yours loves somebody else better or more than they love you, or that a close friend thinks that somebody is a better lover than you are. From their point of view it may be true, but it certainly isn't a universal truth, and it's pretty obvious that nobody benefits from hearing such comparisons.

A lot of recent writing about relationships, particularly from America, suggests that what is really needed for people to get along with one another is a set of agreements. Two people can decide to relate in any way they want, as long as they make agreements about it and stick to them. In many situations agreements are an excellent way of dealing with things. They certainly help to bring clarity into a situation: if you say that you can't stand it if I stay the night with a particular friend and I say I won't, then we have a clear agreement. Agreements make organisation more efficient – as when you and I agree that I will cook tonight and you will cook tomorrow night. Agreements allocate responsibilities: I'll put the children to bed if you'll wash up.

All this is fine in theory, and there is no doubt that in

many situations agreements can work well. But I also think that agreements, especially agreements about relationships, are likely to fail if two things aren't taken into account. The first is that agreements can only realistically be made between people who have both consciously chosen to make an agreement; the second is that agreements must take into account the existing inequalities between people.

Relationships often break down because one partner does not keep, or is thought not to have kept, their part of an agreement. Keeping to an agreement is certainly important, but when the partners look back on the agreement that was made and has now been broken, it's very often clear that when the people and the situation are taken fully into account, it was highly unlikely that the person who broke the agreement could have kept to it. For agreements to work, they have to be freely chosen commitments by both people, and many agreements fail because they are not free and unpressured commitments. Very often one of the people has not consciously agreed at all, or has been forced to agree against the threat of the withdrawal of love and support.

Imagine a ravenous child left alone in a kitchen full of tempting morsels. The phone rings. 'Now I trust you not to eat anything before dinner,' you say, not waiting for the child's answer before you leave. The child didn't agree not to eat anything, though this will probably not stop you being upset by the 'breaking' of the agreement when you return to find fingerprints in the trifle. The 'breaking' of agreements that were never consciously made in the first place, or were left vague, is a pitfall of a great deal of relating too. For instance, if two people get physically close and don't make an agreement that their relationship is physically exclusive, then one can hardly accuse the other of breaking an agreement if they see the other cuddling with a third person. This doesn't mean that they won't have feelings about it, but they can't resort to a non-existent agreement.

Some people think that threats are agreements – 'If I see you with that man again I'll leave you' – but they're not. To leave when you see your partner with that man again is a choice that you can make, but you can't say that your partner broke your agreement. Most threats are much more subtle and involve playing on someone's weaknesses, but agreements obtained under duress aren't freely chosen commitments either. 'Oh all right, I won't see him again. Anything to stop you arguing.'

So the best agreements are the free and conscious choice of both partners, commitments that they feel able to make and follow through. But as well as being the free choice of the participants, agreements have to start from the present situation, and not from some theoretical point of equality. This is the second reason why many agreements fail.

Picture two partners in a relationship. One has always been encouraged to be open and relaxed about sexuality, has had a number of satisfying and intimate sexual friendships, and doesn't feel threatened by their friend's intimate behaviour. The other had a repressive childhood and was often left alone; their early sexual encounters were painful, and they have a deep fear of being rejected and abandoned. These two people decide to have an agreement about how they relate to other people outside their relationship. The first partner suggests that they both trust each other to be intimate with whoever they want, as long as they don't do anything that puts their partner's health at risk and as long as they don't keep secrets from each other. Out of context this might seem a perfectly reasonable agreement; what it doesn't take into account, however, is that the first partner sees no problem at all in choosing to make this commitment, while the second is scared stiff.

People start from different situations and with different experiences. In order to make things work, agreements often need to be unequal in order to take account of the prevailing inequality in the relationship. Thus the agreement that might work in the above situation may be that the first partner would agree to be sexually monogamous for a while to allay the second partner's fears, while the second partner would agree to look deeply at the origins of that fear. Out of context this may now seem an unfair agreement, but it is one that can help and support both partners, that they can both commit themselves to, and that they both feel able to follow through.

This way of looking at the basic inequality of the prevailing situation is very similar to the concept of positive discrimination, where disadvantaged people are given relatively more opportunity in order to compensate for their relative powerlessness. The situation we have just looked at shows how positive discrimination might work in an agreement about shared sexuality, and there are many other situations in which an acknowledgement and understanding of existing inequalities can often help form the basis for agreements designed to help both partners in a relationship to discover their power and freedom.

The two areas that immediately spring to mind are childcare and housework, especially where the sharing of the work is to be allocated between a woman and a man, or between women and men in a group. House and children are usually considered to be women's work while the man leaves home to do the real work, but many people are actively working to break down this pattern, as we shall see in the next chapter.

If a woman and a man agree to share childcare equally, it is a very different experience for the woman than for the man. For the woman it will mean letting go of the traditional woman's role of always being there for the children; for the man it will be letting go of the convenient belief of always knowing that a woman will be there to step in if things get difficult or boring. When a woman and a man agree to share childcare equally, the woman often gets very impatient with the man doing things wrong as he learns (and almost certainly not doing it as well as she can), and the man uses any number of excuses to do as little as possible, knowing that the woman, when it's her turn, will sort out the dirty washing, buy the children's clothes, and help them with their thank-you letters.

The same is true of housework, where women are working against a conditioning that says that housework always takes priority over other things, and men are working against a conditioning that says that housework always has the lowest priority. The acknowledgement of the advantages of positive discrimination in both of these areas suggests that if men are serious about supporting women to have the freedom to choose, they sometimes need to be willing to enter unequal agreements to counteract the basic inequality that currently exists between men and women. There will be circumstances in which, for example, they might offer to do more than half of the childcare and housework in order to give a women a more than equal chance of catching up on missed experiences in other areas.

In this chapter we have looked at the importance of choice, and at some of the things that render people powerless, especially in relationships. Awareness of a situation is very important, but awareness is just part of putting alternatives into practice. If anything is going to change, we need to turn our new awareness into action. Most of us will be able to think of a host of ways in which we would like to change our lives. The problem is often that the changes we would like to make seem so enormous that we can't see any way of achieving them. The main thing to remember is that many small changes add up to big changes, and that individual changes eventually add up to social trends.

All we really have to do is be willing to change, and to decide to make changes that are reasonable and achievable. It might only be smiling at one person every day, having one deep and interesting conversation a week, taking ten minutes every day to read a book. The important thing is to follow through on what we choose to do.

Changing powerlessness to power, and addiction to choice, is the basis of acknowledging that everybody is independent, equal and important. This fundamental understanding helps us to see clearly the radical alternatives to the dependent relationships based on possessive and exclusive love we have been looking at:

❧ The alternative to dependence is interdependence.

❧ The alternative to possessive love is non-possessive love.

❧ The alternative to exclusive love is inclusive love.

It sounds simple and, though it's maybe difficult to believe, it is simple. It means forgetting all the things we have been taught that limit us in the ways we relate to one another.

10

Love's Labours Rediscovered

Most books that look at the present state of human relationships don't devote much space to hopeful developments in relating and the new forms that relating is beginning to take. There is so much to examine and unravel about the way things are that it's not surprising if most authors can only spare a few pages at the end to add a little hope for the future. We've looked at the present state of relating, how it might be improved, and some guidelines for painfree closeness. But if current patterns of monogamy and coupledom, marriage and the family leave a lot to be desired, what might we replace them with which would still supply the important needs they do fulfil, and at the same time overcome their many limitations?

The search for alternatives is not new, though the history of experimental forms of relating is not often recorded, being part of 'private' as opposed to 'public' life. Instead of being seen as an ongoing examination of alternatives with a great deal of interaction and continuity, the movement of people choosing to examine carefully the way they relate to other people and create alternative forms is often represented as a series of failed experiments or social crazes. Many people would like to believe that the communes movement happened in the 1960s and 1970s and is now safely dead, and that feminism happened first with the suffragettes and then again in the 1970s, but both were passing phases and totally unconnected.

Fortunately it isn't true. Not only do the alternatives to conventional ways of relating have a long history, but many practical alternatives exist and are flourishing. An ever-widening and closely-knit international network of co-operative and communal projects is attracting very many people disenchanted with the isolation and dehumanisation of institutionalised living. These people are starting to find a new meaning to personal freedom and choice, and once the freedom is gained it is not easily given up.

So what are the alternatives? Let's look at monogamy and coupledom first, and possible replacements to conventional long-term exclusive intimacy. Sue Cartledge, in an anthology called *Sex and Love*, introduces the problem:

> But with what, exactly, is monogamy to be replaced? Often lifelong monogamy has simply been replaced by serial monogamy; a succession of exclusive relationships ending more or less painfully as a new lover comes on the scene. Conducting more than one sexual relationship at a time does not always solve the problem. It can simply be what has been labelled 'parallel monogamy', where overlapping relationships raise a host of problems of their own. What is the morality of triangular relationships when one partner would prefer monogamy? Are they alone responsible for their pain, suffering because they haven't tried hard enough to destroy their possessiveness? Structuring into 'primary' and 'secondary'

relationships, while it may be a convenient solution for the two halves of the primary, can be agony for the unfortunate secondary lover, condemned to second place by the historical accident of arriving on the scene second. Sexual and emotional jealousy cannot simply be wished away.

The basis of relating must be the acknowledgement of every individual person as an important, independent and free human being, with a range of basic needs. Many of these needs – attention, closeness, touch and support among them – are often most readily fulfilled in one-to-one contact with other people, but nobody's full range of needs, not even all their emotional and physical needs, can ever be fulfilled by one other person, and I think any expectation that they will be is doomed to disappointment.

Instead of going through the different needs that people have, and examining all the problems and limitations of depending on one other person for emotional support, or for help with children, or for mental stimulation, I'll mention just one need that traditional monogamy can never fulfil other than deceitfully and furtively – the need for novelty in relating. To accept monogamy is to deny yourself thereafter the excitement and thrill of experiencing a new intimate friendship, and being able to celebrate it openly, joyfully and passionately.

In her book *On Loving Men*, Jane Lazarre describes the feelings well:

The passion finally was enormous. It was uncontainable. I have never met a woman who experiences sexuality in this depth within a marriage of ten years or more, no matter how much passion she may feel for her husband, no matter with what empathy and precision they have come to know each other's physical needs. It was simply a different order of experience.

She is also very realistic about the problems:

I have no idea how to integrate this insight with the demand for loyalty, the need for abiding relationship that must often be based on exclusivity when sexuality is involved, the destructiveness of lying to a person whom you love and live with and to whom you are unalterably committed in friendship; and yet the equally intense destruction of allowing him to live with the knowledge that you are involved passionately with someone else. I don't know how to untangle the threads of personal need and obligation to others.

The problems of three-way relating that Jane Lazarre describes are difficult ones, but I think it's important to understand and deal with the shortcomings of triangularity, and to see that on the path from monogamy to more inclusive relating the introduction of 'the third person' is only the first, though often the most painful, step.

By 'inclusive relating' I am certainly not suggesting that everybody should immediately feel free to be intimate with everybody they find attractive. The awareness and sensitivity – and the time – that this would require are well beyond our current capacity. What I mean is, and I hope that this is fairly obvious by now, that each of us needs a variety of closeness and friendship. Some of this closeness, particularly if it involves physical intimacy, is bound to threaten the status quo of exclusive coupledom. In a society like ours where coupledom reigns supreme, any move towards inclusivity, whether it involves sexuality or not (though if it does it will almost certainly be more difficult to work through), will have its problems. If it isn't consciously seen as a step towards inclusivity, the introduction of a third person can often be as oppressive as the original coupledom, and may have the added bogeys of manipulation and jealousy thrown in for good measure.

If you are consciously setting out from tight coupledom towards more inclusive relating (and often, as we've seen, even if you're not), at some point the question of the third person is bound to arise. Many sallies into non-exclusivity don't survive the introduction of the third person because the belief that it can never work is so entrenched, and because the 'normal' pattern of coupledom is so fixed. Moving from exclusivity to inclusivity is one of those areas (we looked at some others in the last chapter) where it's vitally important to take account of people's different starting points in order to minimise the pain and suffering described by Sue Cartledge.

In a society where the men in heterosexual relationships are expected to work out in the big wide world and the women to stay at home and look after the children – the most full-time job there is if you're doing it single-handed – it's not at all surprising that men usually have far more opportunity to explore relating outside their coupledom than women do. The additional double standard of condoning 'affairs' for men but not for women creates a sharp inequality of opportunity when it comes to ways of expanding out of coupledom.

If a man and a woman do consciously decide to have a non-exclusive relationship, or to move beyond exclusive monogamy, it has to be done carefully and sensitively, and part of the sensitivity is taking into account the widespread inequality between men's freedom and women's freedom. In order to support a woman to choose her own future, including the way she chooses to relate to other people, a man must be willing to do very practical things like look after the children and the house while their partner goes away from home, to encourage her friendships with other people without judging them or interfering in them, and when necessary to forgo his own exploration of closeness outside the partnership if his partner can't stand the pain it provokes.

Close three-way relationships can be very rewarding, but the potential anguish of dishonesty and non-communication is even greater than in coupledom. The two most common agonies in triangular relationships result from the setting up of one person against another – manipulation – and the fear of competing for love and attention that you feel should be exclusively yours – jealousy.

In her autobiography *The Shame is Over*, the Dutch feminist Anja Meulenbelt describes what happened when she became intimate with a married man, Ton, and then discovered that, contrary to what he was telling her, his wife Anna knew nothing about Anja. An agreement between Anja and Anna to be open and honest between themselves about the three-way relationship showed up Ton's weaknesses, and gradually developed into a close and loving relationship between the two women.

Ton's reaction was to make Anna choose between him and Anja, even though he assumed that it was fine for him to be concurrently intimate with both women. Anja was furious with the way he manipulated Anna:

> I almost choke from suppressed anger, can't get a word out, speechless from so much hypocrisy. Ton always had his mistresses concurrent with his marriage, always left it to Anna to adapt herself. Ton now calls on holy matrimony when Anna, for the first time in her life, is the one who is having another relationship. I hate him as he sits there, gambling on his power position. The power he has to force Anna to choose between him and me.

In the exploration of inclusive relating, indeed in any sort of relating, force and manipulation are guaranteed killers, but even knowing that won't stop people – men usually – using them against other people. The use of manipulation usually arises from a combination of believing that manipulation will work where clarity and reason won't – a vain hope – and being frightened that you're going to lose something.

If manipulation is a painful course of action, jealousy is the painful feeling that often leads to manipulation. It too arises from a fear of losing something, usually someone's love and attention, and, like manipulation, jealousy is self-defeating – the more jealous you feel the more you will feel rejected, breeding ever more jealousy. Convention has it that jealousy is the natural reaction to 'losing someone', which since you can't own them in the first place simply perpetuates the myth of possession we examined in Chapter 7. And as Nena and George O'Neill make clear in their book *Open Marriage*, there is nothing at all natural about jealousy. Jealousy is a learned response, based on a long but misguided romantic tradition, and it has no place in the future of inclusive relating. The feminist activist Emma Goldman, writing in 1906, made it clear what she thought about jealousy: 'All lovers do well to leave the doors of their love wide open,' she wrote. 'When love can come and go without meeting a watchdog, jealousy will rarely take root, because it will soon learn that where there are no locks and keys there is no place for suspicion and distrust, the two elements upon which jealousy thrives and prospers.'

However, calmly denying jealousy a future isn't going to make our problems, pain, hurt, conditioning and feelings concerning inclusive relationships disappear overnight. As Sue Cartledge says, the feelings of sexual and emotional jealousy cannot simply be wished away. Even when you get round to realising that you have the power to choose how you want your relationships to be, you still have to deal with the feelings that arise from being hurt now and in the past, and the suppressed anger, fear and sadness from that hurt. Even when you have chosen your preferred ways of relating, you still have to take into account the other people in your life and how they feel about your choice.

I said earlier that the expansion of coupledom into three-way relating can be just the first step towards inclusive relating, and it's time now to look very practically at what I mean by inclusive relating. Because we all have a wide range of needs, and because everybody is unique and has different needs, I strongly believe that the best way of relating to the people in the world is to have a network of good friends. The network needs to be large enough to fulfil our needs without making excessive demands on any one person, and flexible enough to meet our changing needs. Within their network of friends, everybody needs a group of people they can particularly trust, so that they know that love and attention and support are there for them when they need it.

Many people will find that they already have a network and a trusted support group, but if you haven't you may need to spend some time and effort creating it. You may actually have to say to people: 'Will you be part of my support group?' All sorts of support groups have always existed under different names or no name at all, but in recent years many support groups have been set up by people with particular backgrounds or specific problems: by rape or incest victims; ex-prisoners and single parents; by divorced people; AIDS and cancer sufferers; and Vietnam veterans. Your support group can just as well be the people you live with, your women's or men's group, or some of your neighbours; the important thing is to know that those people will be there for you when you need them.

Now you may feel that a network of close friends isn't the same thing at all as the sort of inclusive relating whose first step is the three-way relating I've been talking about. In a way I can see your point, since when I talk about three-way relating, especially with many of the examples I have given, it isn't clear whether I mean an expansion of monogamy into a wider range of intimate relating, or whether I mean making sure that we have close friends outside our coupledom.

Well, I mean both. In many ways I think it's not particularly relevant whether the choice to expand our ways of relating beyond conventional coupledom includes a sexual element or not. At the same time it's putting a great strain on sexuality (which after all is supposed to be enjoyable) to leave it out of that expansion for ever, especially when sexual monogamy is already an excuse for so much oppressive behaviour, and when such a blatant double standard already exists between men and women concerning shared sexuality outside coupledom.

While inclusive relating opens up possibilities for an infinite variety of friendships, it may well be that in important practical questions such as who you share your house with, who you share childcare with, and who you share your bed with, you may well choose one person to be your especially close friend, even though you may know and relate closely to many others. If you choose one other person to relate to in a special way for particular aspects of your life together, maybe for a long period of time, to most people's eyes there won't appear to be much to distinguish your choice of relating from conventional coupledom.

Although to untrained eyes consciously chosen long-term committed relating to one special friend might seem like coupledom under another name, there is a world of difference between them, a point I shall return to shortly. Yet precisely because it can appear very similar, it's all the more important to be careful not to slip into conventional habits. This is particularly true if you choose to spend time being sexually monogamous; in this case it's important to be very clear that it's the free and unpressured choice of both partners, to be willing to change the arrangement when one of the partners changes their mind (though being sensitive to the needs of the other), and to be very aware that most people will assume, unless you explain otherwise (and even then they'll have problems), that your arrangement is no different from the exclusivity of marriage. Unless you have chosen a same-sex partner, when most people will find it difficult to acknowledge your committed friendship at all.

It's also important to acknowledge that when someone has consciously chosen a special friend to share things with, we can support them in their choice even if it's inconvenient or painful for us, though that certainly doesn't prevent us from expressing our annoyance or sadness. They need to be open to our thoughts and feelings, but the freedom to choose that we looked at in the last chapter must be the freedom to choose the way of relating that is right for each of us, and for each of us that way will be different. At times that same freedom will be the freedom to make mistakes – these are times when we really need our support group.

One way in which people are providing themselves with support groups and a close-knit network of friends is to live communally or collectively. Whether they share a house or live close to each other and share facilities, a rapidly growing number of people are recognising the advantages of living in a larger group than the traditional two-generation blood-related family.

As Eric Raimy describes in *Shared Houses, Shared Lives*, these people have

> made a discovery of great social significance in an era in which people are experiencing a growing sense of isolation. They have discovered that you

don't have to be related by blood or marriage to become part of a warm, supportive household that feels like a family or a miniature community. Their goal is simply to live together in a way that is caring and fun.

Easily said but, like so many challenges of changing lifestyle, not so easily done. Yet large numbers of people all over the world are working out the practicalities of communal living (relearning in many cases, since it isn't so long ago that we forgot how to live communally). Intentional communities and communal projects are alive and well, from California to India, Australia to rural Scotland.

I have already made the distinction between people choosing to share important parts of their life – looking after children together for instance, or living in the same house – and people being together in an unconscious way, following more or less blindly the dictates of convention. I would like to think of this conscious sharing and mutual effort as a committed friendship, and look at what needs to be taken into account in such a friendship.

There are four main elements in committing yourself to special friendship with somebody else, though the commitment is rarely formal and the edges are necessarily indistinct. First is the general commitment to mutual support and acknowledgement, then there is the commitment to the joint care of the projects you are choosing to share, then there is the commitment to the agreements you need to make to ensure that the joint projects work, and finally there is the commitment to work through and attempt to resolve any problems that might arise on the way.

The general commitment in a committed friendship acknowledges that it will be very difficult to undertake a joint project with someone if you don't have a basic agreement to support each other. Among the things that come to my mind when I think of this sort of commitment are that people will acknowledge each other's freedom and choice, give each other love and attention, support each other mentally, emotionally and physically, and be there for each other when they need help. The items in the list will vary from friendship to friendship, but it's much clearer to have at least some idea of what you're committing yourself to rather than entering an important relationship blindly.

The second commitment is to the joint project or projects you intend to share – a house, children, a work project. Different projects need different levels of commitment and different lengths of commitment. Joint parenting, especially if it's only between two people, is a hefty commitment for up to twenty years; sharing a mortgage on a house is a weighty commitment too.

Then there is the commitment to the agreements that will help the project to work, and agreements (taking into account what we talked about in the last chapter) can take many forms. The important things are that agreements are the free and aware choice of everybody involved, and that you only make agreements that you believe you can keep to. Agreements are there to oil the wheels of friendship, not to hit each other over the head with when the going gets tough.

The commitment to working things out, what many people call 'the commitment to process', is crucial if the friendship is to survive everything the world can throw at it. In some ways it's not very different from the 'richer and poorer, in sickness and in health' vow of the wedding ceremony, though it goes a lot further. It means that if the friendship is to grow and flourish, change and be allowed to become whatever it needs to, everything must be open to discussion, exploration and negotiation.

You don't have to be sharing a project before you can

commit yourself in friendship to another person. I have been talking more about long-term committed friendship as an alternative to coupledom – and as we shall see in a minute, as an alternative to marriage – but the general commitment to mutual support comes very soon after the start of any important friendship. Nor does such a commitment have to be formally made, signed and sealed, but it's always reassuring to tell and be told by a friend that there is something special to you both about your friendship.

Committed friendships don't only involve pairs of people. One-to-one friendships are very important, as are the space and privacy to explore and enjoy one-to-one contact, but commitments between friends, whether commitments to mutual support or commitments to a project, can often involve three or more people. Because most of us are not used to inclusive relating, old patterns of rejection, jealousy, guilt, competition and fear (to name but a few) may well arise within the group, but I don't accept that the existence of such feelings, nor the fact that some group friendships don't survive (many marriages don't), as evidence that close group friendships can't be stimulating and fulfilling.

People and their circumstances change all the time, so any replacement of current forms of relating must be flexible enough to take account of change. The need for flexibility doesn't always fit too smoothly with the need for long-term commitment – for example if the other parent of your children decides to live in Outer Mongolia – but it does often help to clarify the issues involved. Since the future is unknowable, particularly the unexpected things that might require us to change our commitments, those commitments cannot specifically allow for changing circumstances. What we can do is be open to and aware of those changing circumstances, be willing to let the commitments change, and be sensitive enough to work out together the least disruptive and painful way of changing the arrangements and commitments to take account of the new circumstances.

I've talked a lot about each person's need for love, support and attention, but when it comes to relating we all have some fairly specific material needs too. Two of the most important are directly related to choice in areas where many people feel they don't have any. The first, as I have already mentioned, is that everybody over the age of about eight or nine ideally needs a room or a space of their own where they can choose to be alone and uninterrupted. The second is that everybody whose choice of relating includes sleeping with other people (whatever your interpretation of 'sleeping') should ideally have their own bed large enough to accommodate two people, so they can choose when they want to sleep with someone else and when they want to sleep on their own. I fully recognise the problems of providing separate space and sufficient large beds in many cases, especially for children. But in a society that puts a roof over cars before it gives everybody their own room, the problem is largely to do with priorities and distribution rather than the inability to provide everybody with their basic needs.

As we saw in Chapter 8, marriage confers society's stamp of approval on a particular and often very limiting way of relating and, if you choose non-conventional ways of relating, one of the things you will have to live without is the approval of those who believe that convention and their reactions are more important than your choice. The Inland Revenue will ask why you don't have the same surname as the other parent of your children; the man from the Department of Social Security will assume that the double bed means that someone of the other sex is sharing your room.

The biggest problem that most people encounter in this area is with their parents, and the fear of upsetting their parents still stops many otherwise independent and mature adults from doing unconventional things, or – even more often – prevents them from telling their parents about the unconventional things they are doing. This isn't very flattering to the parents, since it assumes that the parents are bound to disapprove, and it isn't giving them the option of knowing what's happening in their children's lives. On the other hand, we often refrain from doing things, or do them and refrain from telling our parents, because we know them all too well, and have a good idea that they won't like what they hear.

This sorry state of affairs is the almost inevitable response to an approach to parenting in which children view their parents as controlling and interfering with their lives, the natural reaction to which is to hide from them the things that most engender their displeasure and ridicule. Is it any wonder that we sometimes forget that we can choose to live our own lives now, and don't have to ask mummy and daddy if we can get down from the table?

The solution to this seemingly intractable problem involves sensitivity and willingness on both sides, but probably above all it demands as much honesty as is compatible with maintaining communication. It often includes the healing of old wounds – those of the parents as well as those of the children. Where parents appear to their children as the all-powerful tyrants who manipulated their early lives, it's easy to forget all the good things about them, and a list consisting solely of grievances and complaints about your parents certainly won't help healing and mutual understanding. Finally, if you do everything you possibly can to understand, communicate with and be sensitive to your parents (or your children for that matter), and fail, that's the way it has to be for the time being. Family don't have to be friends.

As well as marking the start of a conventional long-

term intimate relationship, the beginning of a marriage –
the wedding – is also a public statement that a woman
and a man are changing the status of their friendship. It
seems to me that two quite distinct elements have unfortunately become mixed together in the conventional marriage ceremony – one rather limiting and one very joyful.
The limiting element is that two people have set out,
often without realising the pitfalls of marriage and almost
certainly not having looked seriously at the alternatives,
to make what they can of a very constricting institution.
The joyful element is that a commitment to a special and
important friendship is well worth celebrating. Inviting
all your friends to hear you make your commitments,
then singing and dancing and enjoying yourselves together, is an excellent way to mark an important commitment to mutual friendship, shared parenting, or the birth
of a communal project.

Marriage also traditionally provides 'for the procreation of children', and the wedding is seen by many as the
beginning of a new family, since marriage and children,
via the sexuality that has now been legitimised, are
assumed to go hand in hand. Many arguments have been
created to show how the children of any arrangement
other than a traditional two-parent married family are
bound to suffer, but both reason and experience suggest
that where children have their own loving and supportive network of friends, the details of their childcare
arrangements make little difference to the child's
happiness.

In a society where married two-person parenting is
considered to be the only proper way of caring for children, any other arrangement is automatically considered to
be inferior, and it's important to recognise that alternative
arrangements for childcare are difficult because those
who decide how resources are used choose to make them
difficult. As money is diverted away from community

nurseries and day-care centres, single parents, usually women, are deprived of the shared childcare that all children (and all parents) need. Work is usually offered to those who can work full time because somebody else, again usually a woman, is caring for the children; without flexibility in work patterns, shared childcare is extremely difficult to organise.

If our aim is to acknowledge each human being as an important, powerful and independent person, then we have to stop thinking in terms of 'single' parents and 'double' parents. There is nothing magical about the way that two people can look after children, especially when you realise that the majority of children who have two parents are only looked after by one of them – the only incontrovertible fact is that it takes two people to create a child. It may well be (and I think it's a fairly logical arrangement) that the two people who have created the child will share looking after it, but I think it's far healthier to see each of those people as single parents, rather than as a jelly-like lump called 'family' which tends to devalue the individuality of each member and see them as roles instead of as people. Where the unique individuality of people is valued, every parent is a single parent.

A few days ago I was talking to a friend at our local playgroup, and she said 'I think every child needs at least half a dozen parents!' I know what she means. This is the logical extension of acknowledging children as human beings in their own right, and realising that everybody needs a network of friends and a support group. Children too need a network of friends, and I think it's important for that network to include several adults as well as children. This would mean that more people became involved in childcare, and would also mean a shift in many children's patterns of relating away from spending so much of their time with a group of same-age, same-sex friends, which would bring enormous advantages to both adults and children.

Children also need a support group, a function traditionally ascribed to the family. I think it's asking far too much of the two parents of the child to constitute the child's only support group, but convention firmly places that responsibility with parents, and instructs them to treat their children as their property and to be annoyed if anybody else 'interferes' with it. Many people's childhood memories include long periods of loneliness and lack of attention, and much of this is a result of the family not providing, and not realistically being able to provide, the support that every child needs.

I'm not saying that a child's two parents can't provide it with the support, love and attention it needs, but in most families a child often spends an appreciable amount of its life with only one parent, and one other person – as in coupledom – is not enough of a support system for anyone. In general I don't think that two people – the number of supporters a nuclear family provides – are enough either, especially when, as a child, you have no choice about who those people are. While their biological parents will continue to be the basis for most children's support group, I think that every child, from birth onwards, would be happier and more fulfilled if more people were involved in caring for them, and a growing number of 'baby groups' and 'child support groups' are successfully replacing the conventional family as the vital source of love and attention that every child needs.

Many of the alternatives to monogamy and coupledom, marriage and the family, seem difficult to explain and describe, even though they are based on very simple and basic concepts. Some of the apparent difficulty arises because the details of the arrangements vary from situation to situation, but a lot is to do with the question of labelling and naming alternative arrangements. In this chapter I've used terms like 'committed friendship' and

'support group', which could in some people's arrangements replace 'marriage' and 'family'. But it would be
very easy to replace one limiting and oppressive institution with another, and that is not at all what I have in
mind. Neither is it necessary to wait for a label before you
work out how you want to relate, though there is a
tendency within our tidy society to believe that things
without names don't exist.

It's often not easy to see how we get from where we are
to where we'd like to be, and many of the suggestions
I've made may seem unrealistic in the light of current
practice in relating. I often feel pretty pessimistic about
human relations myself, but I also know that in many
little ways, all over the world, people are experimenting
with new forms of relating and are beginning to understand the rewards of freedom, choice and equality in
friendship. If you think my suggestions sound utopian,
you're right. I don't believe that utopian suggestions are
at all unattainable. It seems to me that the only other
choices are stagnation, frustration or despair.

11

The Same Only Different

When so much stress is laid on the identification and exaggeration of every real and imagined difference between women and men, and sex is the biggest skeleton in our cultural cupboard, it is no surprise to find that what most disgusts many people is the idea of two people of the same sex wanting to be sexual friends. The same belief system that limits the variety of sexual sharing to one specific 'act' and the variety of relating to heterosexual coupledom sees homosexuality as a dread perversion and a terrible social disease.

Things are changing for the better, though slowly and with almost as many setbacks as advances. 'I thought men like that shot themselves,' King George V is reputed to have said on learning that a close friend was in a homosexual relationship. I don't know what monarchs think nowadays, but large numbers of people, especially young people and the inhabitants of cities where the gay population is substantial, are today much more tolerant and open-minded about the sexual preferences of their friends and neighbours.

Laws proscribing homosexuality have been liberalised,

though there remains an enormous difference between what is allowed in private and what is considered 'indecent' in public. Same-sex friends holding hands and kissing in public are still regularly charged with breaching the peace – a contradiction in terms if ever there was one. As a result of new British legislation passed in 1987 – the infamous Clause 28 – local authorities are now constrained from doing anything which may be construed as 'promoting homosexuality'. In practice Clause 28 has proved hard to interpret and appears to have had relatively little effect on local government activities, though the ever-present threat of legal action remains.

Then there is AIDS, seen by many people as a 'gay disease'. 'There can be no escape from the fact that AIDS has cut a deep wound through all of the post-sixties' changes in gay consciousness and culture,' writes John Shiers in an essay called 'One Step to Heaven'. 'In America, the home of the specialised sexual fantasy and of recreational sex as a lifestyle, the seventies' generation of new male homosexuals has been precisely those people most affected by the health crisis posed by AIDS. The funeral pyre has replaced the hi-energy music for literally thousands of gay men who have met painful, premature and such senseless deaths.'

Those who fear and loathe homosexuality have used every opportunity to blame the gay community for the appearance and spread of AIDS, and to insist that the disease is nothing more than just punishment for their wicked lifestyle. During the late 1980s the vehemence of this moral backlash succeeded in turning many people against the gay community, reinforcing the image of homosexuals as sad, bad and sick. 'But what has also developed,' continues John Shiers, 'is a new sense of gay solidarity and togetherness, which would have been impossible in the bad old days when fear, guilt and secrecy reigned unchallanged.'

While AIDS and the sexual proclivities of gay men were catching the popular imagination, the spotlight of moral righteousness was also falling on lesbian women wanting to maintain custody of their children. Following three notorious cases in 1975 where lesbian mothers were refused custody in favour of their ex-husbands who had established 'normal relationships', it became clear during the course of the following decade that more than 90 per cent of lesbian mothers were losing their children simply because they were gay. As with gay men and AIDS, the lesbian custody issue has created a widespread sense of solidarity within the lesbian community, and has brought the issues of prejudice and discrimination into the public arena.

While male homosexuality has been outlawed from biblical times onward, lesbianism has hardly been acknowledged even to exist in a male-defined world – the only physical attraction that men allow women to have is towards men. Women have the last laugh because they do it anyway, but the lack of acknowledgement of lesbianism hasn't stopped either the indignation of self-styled upholders of moral virtue, or the harassment and vilification of women who choose to be close to other women. Maureen Colquhoun, a former MP, discovered this to her cost when she expected her colleagues and the media to be at least reasonably sympathetic to her decision to start a committed friendship with another woman. She was wrong. In a hundred subtle, mean and underhand ways she was misrepresented, misquoted, and given no right to reply.

Together with a large and growing number of people, I unreservedly support anybody who wishes to love and care for and be physically intimate with anyone they choose, especially if they are brave enough to ignore one of society's weightiest taboos and love somebody of the same sex. This involves active support for the partners in the friendship, the acknowledgement of both partners as independent and important people, and of their friendship as an important commitment, no more and no less important than any other committed friendship.

The pressure from outraged conventionality sometimes imposes a serious strain on committed same-sex friendships, which demands a lot of support and understanding from both the partners and from their other friends. This support is often difficult to give, since everybody has been bombarded with 'heterosexual-is-normal-and-homosexual-is-disgusting' propaganda for so long. Even when we have recognised the stupidity and oppressiveness of the propaganda, we still have to deal with our carefully nurtured fear of homosexuality, and with the reality of a heavily defended heterosexual society.

While we may support our gay friends, are we prepared to look at what stops more people – including ourselves, if we don't have close same-sex friends – from getting close to people of the same sex? There's a very big gap between the rational acceptance of people's choice to relate to whoever they want to, and the practical work of dismantling the emotional barriers that prevent us from getting close to same-sex friends.

Ever since homosexuality became a suitable subject for doctors and psychiatrists to study, especially in the 1950s, numerous theories have been developed to 'explain' homosexuality. The introductory chapter of a book called *The Theory and Practice of Homosexuality* lists so many that I stopped counting at a hundred. All the researchers seem to have the same problem – they ask 'What causes homosexuality?' and find it very difficult to come up with an answer. They nearly always give an explanation that is vague if not meaningless, and succeed only in proving to their own satisfaction what they believed all along. In fact it's more devious than that, because doctors and psychologists have a considerable interest in finding 'problems' which then need their professional treatment and therapy.

But what if these learned professionals had all the time been asking the wrong question or, worse still, had been asking a question that was totally irrelevant? I think it would be useful to look at why they feel they need to ask that particular question, and then to look at attitudes to relating that follow directly from the sex-role socialisation I talked about in Chapter 4.

When we look at human behaviour we can ask 'Why?' about anything, but what tends to happen is that when something is considered to be totally 'normal' the question is rarely asked: the 'Why?' is aimed only at the 'deviant' behaviour. In our society it's considered normal that men never cry; thus the immediate reaction to a man who can't stop crying is to ask 'Why is he crying?', when we could much more usefully ask 'Why can many men never cry?' We ask 'Why do people go mad?' instead of asking 'What stops anyone and everyone from going mad?'

Once the behaviour has been classified as 'deviant', 'perverted' or 'abnormal', it becomes very difficult to rescue it. Once deviancy becomes part of the experts' stock-in-trade, the concepts that prop up the rickety structure are never again questioned for fear of the whole thing collapsing. Doctors and psychiatrists think they know what they mean by 'normal' and 'deviant', 'heterosexual' and 'homosexual', but they don't.

The reason why they don't know is that, apart from distinctions that are irrelevant when it comes to looking at important things like people and friendship, they are trying to define things that are fundamentally indefinable. Yes, there are differences between women and men which enable us to distinguish homosexual friendship from heterosexual friendship, but if it weren't for all the differentiations that human beings have chosen to make between men and women, and the separation, fear, oppression and discrimination that follow, the homosexual/heterosexual distinction would be about as important as whether we prefer tea or coffee for breakfast. As for the distinction between 'normal' and 'deviant' and all the facile arguments that follow from it, there is no such thing as normal. Any research that starts, however unawarely, from the assumption that there is such a distinction is doomed to instant meaninglessness.

In her book *Wedlocked Women*, Lee Comer sums up the paradox of love and hate that links gender-segregated childhood with the heterosexual romance that people look for in coupledom and marriage:

> Any dance around society reveals that the sexes are placed on opposite poles, with an enormous chasm of oppression, degradation and misunderstanding generated to keep them apart. Out of this, marriage plucks one woman and one man, ties them together with 'love' and asserts that they shall live in harmony, and that they shall, for the rest of their lives, bridge that chasm with a mixture of betrayal, sex, affection, deceit and illusion.

You may remember from Chapter 4 that as a result of early sex-role segregation, 98 per cent of eleven-year-old children have as a best friend someone who is the same sex as they are, and the vast majority of middle school-age children tend to play only with children of their own sex. Thus it is hardly surprising that at the age when teenagers want (or are taught that they want) contact with the other sex, they know next to nothing about the way in which their potential other-sex partners see the world.

The first result is a total lack of understanding. Since the boy (a silly word to use really of a fifteen- or sixteen-year-old) is expected to make the advances, and the girl/woman to receive or reject them, he is often the first to feel hurt and misunderstood. The woman is more likely to be baffled by the seriousness and pretension of the advance. Bewildered by her reactions to unsubtle and inept advances, the man turns to his men friends to commiserate and discuss the problem of getting a woman. The woman, being aware if only subconsciously of the contrivance and double-thinking of the way the sexes are supposed to meet, seeks out her female friends to ponder the futility of sex and the selfishness and insensitivity of men.

Even at this stage many of the problems of misunderstanding could be helped if the two now made a concerted effort to communicate and sympathise, but their fifteen years of sex-role socialisation tells them that this is the way things have to be – men and women are just made like this – and that the only way to help matters is for the man to become more self-assured and assertive and the woman to be less demanding and more accepting.

He decides, with the help of his friends, to show her that he is the sort of man who knows what he is doing as far as sex is concerned. She has been reading *Jackie* and *Company*, and knows that sex is important in a real relationship. Inevitably the worst fears of both of them are fulfilled. When they finally get the opportunity to be sexual together they are not only dissatisfied and confused, but can't understand what went wrong. The woman feels used: receptivity and passivity are all very well, but what happened to love and gentleness? The man feels misunderstood; he did his best to make it good for her but nobody can wait that long.

Time goes on, and after several more-or-less similar experiences the woman probably decides that men will never really understand her and the physical attention she would like. Her real company comes from her close

women friends – she tells them things she wouldn't
dream of telling a man. The man comes to the conclusion
that women are just like that and he'll never understand
them. So he keeps company down at the pub with his
own friends. As Stevi Jackson makes clear in her book
Childhood and Sexuality:

> Children in our society grow up wary of the oppo-
> site sex. Long before this mutual suspicion is
> incorporated into sexual relationships, they learn to
> conform with ideals of femininity and masculinity
> that would make it difficult enough for them to like
> and trust each other even if power, male dominance
> and female subordination did not enter the picture.'

Women and men in our society frequently inhabit
quite different worlds of experience. While a woman may
know something of the male world through supporting
and servicing the men in her life, most men know virtually nothing of the real world of women, and benefit both
materially and emotionally from this ignorance. This life-
long polarisation breeds a real fear of the unknown 'opposite' world: I can't imagine that there is any man who
can truthfully say that he has no fear of women, or any
woman who has no fear of men.

Thus rather than asking 'Why do people have intimate
homosexual relationships?', the more logical question
seems to be 'How can a woman and a man ever get close
enough and understand and trust each other enough to
have a high-quality intimate heterosexual relationship?'
Seen in this light, homosexuality might seem the easy, if
not the obvious, way out. As Anja Meulenbelt says in *For
Ourselves*:

> We don't care a damn how it came about. How it's
> caused is only interesting if you want to be 'cured',
> or if we think we need an excuse – that we really

can't help it and will people please tolerate us. No one thinks they need to explain how heterosexuality is caused. Do you (as a woman) start loving men because of bad experiences with women in your childhood, or because you were seduced by a man before you could develop your normal homosexuality?

In the same way as masculinity and femininity are firmly and indelibly stamped into our consciousness with little chance of us choosing later to transcend the limitations they impose and become fully human, the choice between heterosexual and homosexual relating almost immediately becomes a limiting label. It slots us into a filing drawer with little chance of reclassification or cross-referencing. Once you've chosen, that's it – labelled for life. Anyone who has once chosen to be intimate with a same-sex friend, and has 'gone public' on it, finds it hard to be labelled anything other than 'homosexual', with all that that implies.

If – like heterosexuality – homosexuality isn't fixed and immutable, then at some level of consciousness it must be chosen. I'm well aware that many gay people 'have always known' they were gay, believing that they could have chosen no other way of intimate relating. Other people 'have always known' that they want to work with children, or to serve God, and I see these sorts of choices, these deeply-held convictions, as being of similar validity. This isn't to belittle the choice to be gay. Homosexuality as a personal choice arising from a deep sense of self-knowledge has every right to be acknowledged and respected. Nor is it saying that gay people aren't really gay: they are just as 'really' gay as any straight person is 'really' heterosexual.

If homosexuality is chosen, at whatever level of awareness, it must be possible to keep choosing, and to choose differently every time – if we want to. There are many reasons why we choose to relate as we do, and they change all the time, which is part of why our friendships change all the time. Being homosexual is not like being black or being a woman: it isn't an intrinsic quality of some people and not of others. Even though doctors and psychiatrists may have labelled us, and even though it often seems easier not to believe it, the choice to start an intimate friendship with somebody of either sex is a current preference, not a genetically determined certainty.

Thus 'homosexuality' or 'heterosexuality' most accurately describes the current state of your way of relating. Despite popular usage, a lesbian or a homosexual is not so much someone who without exception prefers shared sexuality with somebody of the same sex, as someone whose current preference is to relate intimately only with people of the same sex. This doesn't mean that you can't choose to be intimate with same-sex friends all the time, but you do – however remote the possibility may seem – always have the choice.

Another favourite research question is to estimate how many gay people there are in the population. It seems to be rising all the time – ten years ago a common guess was one in twenty, now it seems to be one in five. I think this question is pretty irrelevant too. I suppose it is theoretically possible to count the number of people who currently have sexual same-sex friendships, and I suppose too it would be possible to ask people whether their current preference in an intimate relationship is for a same-sex or other-sex partner, though the results would be all but meaningless.

In the sort of society I like to envisage we would be just as likely to have a woman or a man as a close friend, and since we shall be closer to our friends mentally, emotionally and physically, many of our current distinctions between heterosexual and homosexual behaviour will start to evaporate. The layers of limitation, repression and misconception are far too thick for us to know whether we shall in the end find any biological kernel of a reason why, even in a totally non-sexist society, women tend to be attracted to men and vice versa, but I suspect there isn't one, and it's much healthier not to be expecting to find it. Apart from the biology of procreation we can't afford to take anything for granted.

So why label ourselves and thereby exclude from our lives the possibility of intimacy with half of our friends? Either label – heterosexual or homosexual – is equally limiting. Because it's believed to be the 'normal' way of sharing sexuality, most people who consider themselves to be heterosexual don't feel they have to label themselves, but they just as effectively limit themselves. Research suggests that most of us have experienced some sort of homosexual closeness in our lives, so it's hypocritical to believe that heterosexuality is the only means of sexual expression for all times and all places. In order to fight discrimination and narrow-mindedness the gay movement has had to be more overt, and in the process to label itself. But in the very process of labelling the invisible doors tend to slam shut, and for many professed gays the opportunity of also relating intimately with someone of the other sex rarely arises.

There is no doubt that a committed same-sex relationship can be every bit as satisfying and supportive as a committed heterosexual relationship – often more so, since the agreements that make it work are likely to have been made more consciously. Having the same sort of background – including being the same sex – can help a relationship enormously. Yet committed same-sex intimacy will not necessarily 'cure' any of the problems found in same-sex relating. The same process that isolates and oppresses people in heterosexual relationships can just as easily create barriers between men and men, and between women and women, and many of the problems of heterosexual relating cross over into same-sex relating without batting an eyelid.

It's also easy to forget that people in close same-sex friendships still have to work out how to relate to the other-sex people in their lives. It's important to remember that the 'homosexual' label usually only applies to one aspect of somebody's life. People's lives don't only consist of intimate relationships, and most people have worked out how to live with the rest of the world pretty well whatever their sexual preference. As Amanda Sebastyen says on behalf of many lesbians:

> We seem to have no language to express engagement with brothers, sons, lovers, male friends or workmates that doesn't also express compromise with their power. And so uncompromising feminists will tend to stick to a separatist rhetoric which leaves out whole areas of their lives but at least declares 'no surrender'.

Male and female homosexuality are often linked together as a single phenomenon with a single cause, but, although as oppressed groups fighting what appear to be similar battles there are parallels, there are also important differences. There have been many attempts to establish organisations for homosexuals of both sexes, and more often than not they find that the objectives of the men and the women are not the same at all, and either the organisation splits into two groups or some very deep and searching work has to be done within the group. Although there can be a great deal of mutual understanding and support, men and women often have very different reas-ons for ignoring society's pressure for people to relate hetero-sexually.

The motives and reasons for preferring to be intimate

with someone of your own sex are many and varied, and whoever you choose – male or female – I'm sure the main reason is nearly always that you are really attracted to that other person. At the same time, an increasing number of women have decided that the many problems involved in living with and relating to men are just not worth the effort, and that living with other women has enormous advantages. Those who have themselves chosen to invest in conventionality often like to imagine such women as having terrible hang-ups about men and sex. Problems and issues around men there may be, but such a choice is often a reasoned one, based on long experience of men's difficulties in forming loving, non-possessive, egalitarian relationships.

In *The Shame is Over*, Anja Meulenbelt describes her experience like this:

> I used to find men attractive because they helped me to do the things I couldn't otherwise do. Now that I don't use other people in order to get on, but have made my own life, my own work, and can't imagine that I would want someone else's life, I am no longer seeking someone who can offer me something which I can't achieve on my own. I am not asking to be completed, made whole. I am attracted to equals, to people who are emotionally close to me. And they are, on the whole, women. So for me, being a lesbian is about more than sex. It's about loving yourself, recognising how much women can give each other, how strong we can be together. It's about another kind of living, another kind of human relationship.

The decision to live in all-women houses, or to relate intimately to other women, frequently follows directly from the belief, directly related to first-hand experience, that women need to come together in an unthreatening and egalitarian environment in order to rediscover and experience their strength and freedom.

Men can of course form loving, non-possessive and egalitarian same-sex relationships too, and men working out how this fits in with society's views about homosexuality can be just as threatened as their lesbian counterparts. Yet patterns of male homosexuality are in many ways different from lesbian relationships. There are as many varieties of gay intimacy as there are gay partnerships, but while lesbianism is most often seen by lesbians in terms of friendship and solidarity, male homosexuality is seen by many gay men largely in terms of sexual encounter. For many lesbian women their primary choice is to live with and share the company of other women, and the co-operation and warmth that come from mutual closeness and support often includes shared sexuality. Many men experience same-sex friendship in a similar context, where shared sexuality has been part of an intimacy on many levels. More often than in lesbian relationships, however, male homosexuality emphasises genital sexuality – a lot of it with a lot of different partners.

Another important difference between the same-sex intimate friendships of women and men is to do with closeness and trust. Doctor C.A. Tripp, the author of *The Homosexual Matrix*, has a lot to say about 'the male bond'. 'Nothing,' he says, 'has as much value as the sharing of accomplishments with other men. A man's wife may congratulate him, but nothing she can say or do will reverberate inside his pride-chamber as will the reliving of an experience in the minds of other men.' He calls the clubbiness of men 'male bonding', something he claims doesn't happen with women.

From my experience, close and trusting one-to-one friendships between men where competition and rivalry are totally absent are very rare, certainly much rarer than similar friendships between women. Men's closeness is very much to do with the sharing of achievements and skills, and only rarely provides the emotional support that is a key element of most friendships between women. Doctor Tripp's 'male bond' gives men a supposedly biological ('we can't help it') reason for leaving the women in his life to look after housework and children while he goes out to 'bond'. In sanctifying the 'male bond', the way women relate to one another tends to be devalued and belittled.

All of this makes it very difficult for men to relate closely on the level of feelings and emotions. This is, I think, why so much is invested in the physical encounter, and since in the generally accepted model of sexuality intimate physical encounter equates with stimulation to orgasm, many gay men feel that they have little other choice in the way they relate to each other physically.

Male homosexuality has been outlawed far more vigorously than lesbianism. While in general British society allows women to touch each other in public, to hug and to link arms (though not to kiss or hold hands – that would be too much), for men to even touch each other in public has carried the ever-present threat of aggression and harassment. This inevitably leads to male same-sex intimacy being driven into privacy. The day when men can unselfconsciously dance together or stroke one another's hair in public without connotations of homosexuality are still far off, while in many circles women being similarly intimate are totally accepted.

The enormous difference between most lesbian friendships and most gay male friendships reflects the almost universal difficulty that men have in emotionally supporting and physically nurturing other people, especially other men. As Paula Jennings says clearly in *Love Your Enemy?*, 'Men must learn to nurture each other, and if they can't then I don't believe they will survive. I know some men are nicer than others but I've never met one yet who was able to give and receive emotional support to or

from another man.' I think that at last things are beginning to change as a few men glimpse what support and
comfort and warmth men could give each other, but
generations of conditioning work against the process.

The deep belief that men don't have feelings, and
certainly shouldn't show that they have, makes it very
difficult for men to acknowledge any shared emotional
life at all. The only emotional support that most men
receive comes first from their mother and then from their
wife, and the idea of men crying on each other's
shoulders or telling one another about their personal lives
is quite beyond the average man's imagination. It
certainly doesn't fit in with the world of business or
commerce, or the world of pints, darts and football.

The only socially 'acceptable' outlets for a man's emotions are through anger and violence, thus persuading
(male) social anthropologists of the 'naturalness' of male
aggression, but this is a very sorry conclusion to come to.
Violent anger is the only outlet for men's feelings about
anything, while the less destructive channels of crying or
shouting or shaking are closed, leaving men frustrated
without knowing why, and convinced against every
proof to the contrary that they are real men and therefore
don't have feelings.

When things go wrong for little boys, mummy is the
one person who can usually be guaranteed to provide the
comfort and warmth that help to heal the hurt. But there
comes a time for most boys when being big and strong
means that you think you don't need mummy any more.
So you cut off all the comfort you've ever had, and push
the feelings underground, where they rumble around
unfelt until, lo and behold, you find a surrogate mummy
and marry her.

On the other hand, it's totally acceptable for girls to
continue to go to mummy for comfort, and thereafter
women receive most of their emotional support from

other women, who share the same experiences and can understand and sympathise. This vital exchange and closeness is exactly what most men miss; thus when a man sees women enjoying closeness together, the feelings (unacknowledged, of course, since this is a real man) are often of jealousy and rejection, and the reaction is to belittle the contact by labelling it as gossip.

Yet this is exactly the sort of emotional support that men need but rarely acknowledge. When men do need emotional support it is the women in their life that they turn to, and, since emotion is a very private and embarrassing admission, it's usually one woman – the other half of the couple – who bears the brunt. Not surprisingly, as women become aware that they are providing the emotional support for the entire population, especially for men who don't acknowledge or appreciate it, many are rebelling against the built-in unfairness of a society that expects women to do all the emotional work.

If men find it impossible to support and nurture each other emotionally, physical warmth is even rarer. Men hugging each other or a man stroking another's hair are activities currently out of the question for all but a handful of men, and then usually only if they have chosen to come out as gay. Our sex-oriented view of closeness being what it is, physical warmth between men is probably a good deal rarer than gay genital sexuality. No wonder that men shy away from physical closeness with other men – the thoughts of being sexual with another man, of being labelled gay, of being found out, are terrifying. Within the male gay community itself, the idea of 'only' being warm and close and not being sexual is little acknowledged, which makes a big difference between most male gay and most lesbian friendships.

Of all the fears that men have about homosexuality, probably the worst – aside from the very real threat of AIDS – is that they might be considered effeminate. Doctor

Tripp devotes a whole chapter of *The Homosexual Matrix* to a discussion of the psychology of effeminacy, trying desperately to work out why men want to be like women – can it really be to do with cathectic expenditure or the hysterical aggressive response? He's by no means the only one. Mark Cook and Robert McHenry, in *Sexual Attraction*, link homosexuality with effeminacy, and so does the popular imagination.

The sad thing about all this is that most men have very little concept of how most women do behave, as is made clear when men impersonate women yet adopt all the most stereotypical and affected traits that limit women, from high heels to permed hair. The other sad thing is that men don't acknowledge the valuable experiences and insights that women have to offer to us all. Very simply put, the pity is that more men *don't* behave like women – though like strong and loving, powerful and caring women, rather than the pathetic image that many men have of contemporary femininity.

Men have to learn how to be in touch with and share their feelings, and how to be warm, supportive and nurturing to other people – men, women and children. And since men nurturing men is the least practised art it needs the most attention. There's no point pretending that it will be easy for men to feel feelings that have been suppressed for years, and it takes perseverance for a man to relearn how to cry and be comforted by *anybody*, let alone another man. But neither will support and warmth between men improve only by talking about it; at some point we have to take the plunge and do it.

12

The Words We Use

Most of us have grown up with a strong belief that words describe very definite and specific things, and that the connection between words and things are fixed. This is the world of scientific impartiality and objective reality. But it's easy to forget that people created the words in the first place; people divided up their experience of the world to try to understand it. Having divided things up and given them names, those names then not only open up possibilities of description and imagination; they also, unless we are very careful, limit the way we see the world. This is nowhere more true than in the area of relationships and sexuality.

The ability to create language is a basic human attribute but, since men have dominated history, defining language has been almost exclusively a male preserve. And it shows. Let's look, for example, at that simple word 'man'. In Early English 'man' meant a person of either sex, as an entry in the *Anglo-Saxon Chronicle* for the year 639 demonstrates when it describes the Princess Ercongota as 'a holy and wonderful man'. Even in 1752 David Hume, the Scottish philosopher, could write about 'men, both male and female', but by then the parallel practice of male grammatical supremacy had already crept in. Thomas Wilson in 1553 believed that it was more natural to place the man before the woman (as in 'male and female' or 'husband and wife'); Joshua Poole in 1646 wrote that the male was 'the worthier gender', and in 1850 an Act of Parliament created the legal framework for the word 'man' to include women – a Parliament that was composed entirely of men.

Yet although the word 'man' supposedly embraces 'woman', it is perfectly clear that the use of 'man' to include women only applies in a very general way. The supposed comprehensiveness of 'man' hides the fact that it is not truly comprehensive, as can be seen in the title of a research report entitled *Development of the Uterus in Rats, Guinea Pigs and Men,* (quoted by Casey Miller and Kate Swift in *A Handbook of Non-Sexist Writing*). Nobody would talk about Margaret Thatcher as the first female man to become Prime Minister of Great Britain, though a survey of 'Political Man in the Twentieth Century' could hardly ignore her.

Invisibility is but one result of the almost exclusively male formulation of language. Throughout our language – both the words we use often and the way we use them – there is a consistent bias which favours men and traditionally male activities, and degrades women and their activities. The many ways in which this bias operates have been looked at in some detail by Robin Lakoff in *Language and Woman's Place* and by Dale Spender in *Man-Made Language*.

There are many ways in which words either take on negative connotations when they are used to describe women, or where supposedly parallel descriptions allow negative implications to be attached to the female term. The negativity attributed to descriptions of women is often linked with sexual implications, strengthening the male fantasy that anything they dislike or feel threatened by in women can be demeaned by adding sexual innuendo. Robin Lakoff gives an example of the same word, 'professional', used of men and women, with very different implications. 'He's a professional' implies that he has a profession, knows what he's doing, is in charge. 'She's a professional' usually means she's a prostitute.

As soon as words start to be used mostly in relation to women, they begin a seemingly inevitable slide towards derogation and sexual debasement. 'Slut' originally meant a woman or man who looked untidy, 'harlot' was simply another word for 'rogue' or 'rascal', and a 'wench' was a child, used of both girls and boys. Similar words that have become associated with men, like 'fellow' and 'bloke', have maintained their social standing. The process can happen very quickly: 'lesbian' and 'liberated' have taken only a few years to enter male vocabulary as negative and snide putdowns of women's power.

Where there are female and male words that are usually assumed to describe the same situation and standing, it is clear that while the male title has rarely lost any of its power and positivity, the female 'equivalent' has frequently been given (or did it always have?) negative and sexually dubious connotations. Compare, for example, 'witch' and 'wizard', 'mistress' and 'master', 'courtesan' and 'courtier', or 'bitch' and 'dog'.

The female equivalent of 'lady' (a woman of high rank) to the male 'lord' is a fascinating example of this process. The need for a general word for a woman arises largely because the word 'woman' itself has been given subtle undertones of rudeness and negativity. I remember my granny telling me to talk about 'ladies' rather than 'women', with the implication that to call a woman a woman was vaguely insulting. The alternative that most men (and many women) use to describe women who are younger than 'ladies' is 'girls', which at the same time belittles younger women and leaves no special word for female children.

Because of the male bias in language, there is often no

term for women's experience of male behaviour towards women, thus denying women's experience of that behaviour and making it easy to ignore a woman's point of view. Thus there is no woman-defined equivalent for the experience of penetration during sex – there is only the passive 'being penetrated', which perpetuates the belief that a woman's natural role in sex is passive.

When Freud decided that women's emotional problems were mostly to do with penis envy, he ignored the possibility that the source of the problem could be to do with men's envy of women's productive power, and named the explanation he had discovered from his own, male, point of view. Rather than penis envy being the cause of sexual problems, from a woman's point of view the man's problems are much more likely to arise from womb envy. Here is a bathtime conversation between two four-year-olds, recorded by Dale Spender in *Man-Made Language*:

Girl: What's that?
Boy: It's my dicky.
Girl: What do you do with it?
Boy: It's for peeing with.
Girl: Doesn't it get in the way?
Boy: Yes. And it hurts if it gets hit. I have to look after it a lot.
Girl: Can't you tuck it up somewhere?
Boy: No, I've tried, but there's nowhere for it to go.
Girl: Doesn't seem much good to me.
Boy: It's for other things too.
Girl: What else can you do with it?
Boy: My mother says I can help to make babies with it.
Girl: I think your mother's having you on. I don't think it will work.

As we have seen, there are many ways in which our supposedly impartial language incorporates many limiting assumptions about women and men. But what can we do to change the situation?

The first thing is to stop pretending that language is neutral, to learn to look carefully at the language we use, and to be aware of the implications of what we are saying. The upholders of the status quo will tell us that being too fussy about the words we use will make us less fluent, will take a lot of the subtlety and fun out of our communication, and will impoverish the language. To my mind the gain in clarity that follows from increased awareness far outweighs any oppressive right that people feel they should have to put other people down thoughtlessly and spontaneously.

As we become aware of the bias of language, we will often realise that formal dictionary terms will not cover some of our experience of the world, and this is particularly true, as we have seen, of women's experience. In a culture where words carry so much weight, the ability to name something and the power to introduce that name into common usage have become very important, especially to people whose ideas have not traditionally been considered worth taking notice of. The naming of a phenomenon allows it to exist – recent examples of this process include the naming of 'feminism', 'patriarchy', 'sexism' and 'the green movement'. When Betty Friedan was researching her book *The Feminine Mystique* in the early 1960s, her most important discovery was that the feelings of isolation experienced by many suburban women, though widespread, had no name, and could therefore conveniently be ignored.

Widespread awareness of and dissatisfaction with the oppression of women – like the rapidly growing realisation of the need to work for planetary health and against environmental destruction – have gained enormous strength from the process of naming. Feminism and the green movement are here to stay, to identify with, and to provide strength for people who now know that their experiences are not only real and shared but, through being part of our everyday language, are difficult for anybody to ignore.

The naming of experience, and even the general acceptance of those names, does not prevent people with power and authority from denying and belittling the experience. There are many ways of putting an idea down; our language is so carefully constructed around accepted ideas of competition, criticism and innuendo that there is no shortage of linguistic weaponry. You can deny the existence of the phenomenon – 'There is no women's movement, just a few dissatisfied vegetarian housewives who write poetry and don't get enough sex.' You can belittle the ideas by manipulating the names given to them and attaching your own negativity to those names – 'women's libbers', 'veggie nuts', 'ecofreaks'. And the power of words is such that it's often difficult to remember that our experience is unique: if other people's words don't fit our experience then we have the right to name it to our own satisfaction.

We don't have to accept the names and definitions – and values – of people with totally different experience when they try to tell us what our experience is. We can create new words if we want to, though we need to remember that unless the words are only for us, the purpose of language is communication. We need to be able to give clear examples of what our new words mean, especially if we would like a wide range of people with different experiences to understand us.

One of the problems of naming is that of falling into the same trap of linguistic inflexibility that tends to limit all words once they have been created. Once you've named something you tend to limit it, and this is particularly true of descriptions of human behaviour, where the edges between different ways of being are very indistinct, and where the connections and relationships between people are at least as important as the descriptions of individual people.

The language of relating is notoriously vague, and especially when we start to make close contact with somebody else, conventional behaviour often only gives us a choice between embarrassed silence and embarrassed verbal triviality. The vagueness shows itself in every aspect of relating. First we need to sort out for ourselves how we want to relate to somebody else, and it helps if we are able to put it into words for our own clarification. Then it helps if we can tell the other person what we want our relationship with them to be. Lastly, and often the most problematic, other people need some way of labelling our relationship, partly so that they can relate it to themselves and partly so they can describe it to yet other people.

The imprecision of the language of relating shows itself most clearly when it comes to describing how you are relating closely to another person. Let's look at the choices you have:

❧ You can choose descriptions usually reserved for close friendships between young people – boyfriend, girlfriend, dating, 'going out together', 'going steady'.

❧ You can 'get off with' or 'get it together with' someone.

❧ You can use the conventional labels of engagement and marriage – fiancé and fiancée, husband and wife.

❧ You can have an affair, or 'a bit on the side'.

❧ You can use descriptions that also describe the way other animals behave sexually, like 'partner' and 'mate'.

❧ You can be 'a couple'.

❧ You can be 'lovers', having 'a relationship'.

❀ You can invoke spiritual concepts, and be 'soulmates', a 'dyad', or embark on 'the path of two'.

❀ You can have 'a very special friend', or 'someone I live with'.

Despite the apparent variety of describing intimate relationships, these descriptions all have the same built-in shortcomings that are inherent in conventional patterns of relating, which is not surprising, since both behaviour and language are rooted in the same cultural soil.

Not one of these descriptions states precisely the sexual involvement in the relationship – 'lovers' or 'having an affair' are probably the closest to a frank statement of sexual activity, though I find it a bit sad that the love-equals-sex convention is so entrenched in this use of the word 'lover'. On the other hand, shared sexuality is implicit in all these descriptions, which makes it difficult to describe any close relationship (especially, things being as they are, a close heterosexual relationship) without your audience assuming a sexual element.

Many of these descriptions assume a state of exclusive coupledom, and most of them imply such a state. The exception is 'having an affair', with its implications of dishonesty and secrecy, again reinforcing the 'normality' of exclusive monogamy but with the double standard of tacit social approval. 'Having a bit on the side' is a telling description, because it only makes sense if you know what the bit is on the side of, and it's very clear that it can only be on the side of sexual coupledom, like tomato sauce on the side of a plate of chips. Coupledom still reigns supreme.

I find it fascinating how the 'naturalness' arguments for coupledom find expression not only in the biological pair-bonding concepts that lie behind the 'partner' and 'mate' descriptions of relating, but more recently behind certain 'spiritual' concepts of relating. Plato believed that human beings were all in search of the one person who would perfectly complement them, and this idea of 'soul-mates' has recently reared its head again, notably in North America. It's a tricky concept to analyse, because it's difficult to separate out the experience of knowing that you have an affinity with and a mutual attraction towards somebody else from the apparent inevitability of meeting your soulmate – or the other half of your dyad, as psychologist John Lilley calls it. To me, knowledge and choice are equally important, and it disturbs me when people tell me that 'they just knew from the first moment that they should be together'.

If we have little useful language for describing our relationships, the available ways of describing our sexual behaviour are even more limited. Wayland Young, in his book *Eros Denied*, quotes a sixteenth-century Italian, Pietro Aretino, who summed up the romantic tradition's convoluted expressions for fucking in a formidable list: 'key in the lock, pestle in the mortar, nightingale in the nest, dibble in the ditch, pump in the balloon, sword in the sheath . . .' and so on and on and on. You may think things are better today. If so, try this: 'Then his arms tightened about her again and she moved luxuriously as their bodies locked together, and together they sought the farthest shores of desire and fulfilment.' Perhaps you understand the details of what actually happened in this scene from the end of Valerie Sherwood's romantic bodice-buster *This Loving Torment*. I don't.

How do we convey to somebody the idea that we would like to explore sexual intimacy with them? The most common choice is, I'm sure, a meaningful silence full of meaningful gropes and groans, with the occasional, if you're lucky, 'Do you want to, you know . . .?' Not that aware and passionate non-verbal sensuality can't be stimulating and exciting, but especially during early sexual encounters, when communication about

198   Getting Closer

feelings and preferences is the most necessary, words are important too. So what are the options? There really aren't many:

* 'Shall we sleep together? Would you like to stay the night?'

* 'Shall we make love?'

* 'Shall we have sex, fuck, screw (or whatever words you use)?'

* 'Do you fancy having it off/a quick tickle/a toss in the hay (or any number of Aretino-style euphemisms)?'

Getting into details is even more difficult, because the right words don't seem to exist, or they all have subtle innuendoes that we don't necessarily intend. How do you say clearly and lovingly: 'I'd like to spend the night in bed with you, and I think I'd quite like it if you stroked me all over and maybe put your hand on my genitals, but I don't think I want an orgasm and I definitely don't want intercourse'? I only know one way, and that's to say it, but you have to be pretty clear and assertive in order to remain as clear as this during a close encounter.

Where does the vagueness of the language of relating come from? Why can't we use language as sensitively and clearly in the field of human relations as we seem to be able to elsewhere?

A lot of the problem is to do with ideas about the normality of certain ways of relating, which is the reflection in our language of the limitations we looked at in earlier chapters. Where heterosexual exclusive couple-dom, and more specifically marriage, is the only accepted way of being intimate, everything else is discouraged and disparaged. Alternatives aren't allowed to exist, and thus aren't named. It's not just that the language of relating is vague; outside conventional arrangements the words just don't exist to describe our close relationships.

The other side of the normality-of-coupledom argument is, as we have already seen, that any words we do use to describe our relationships will automatically be interpreted by most people to be describing the 'normality' of marriage-like coupledom. As soon as words to describe alternatives are created they very rapidly become to most people just another way of describing the same thing, and this will continue to happen as long as marriage is considered to be the standard against which all relationships are measured.

Another aspect of the language of relating is that as long as sex and intimacy are considered to be very private matters, outside the realm of public debate, the words we use to describe intimate behaviour will not be publicly acceptable. There are several mechanisms at work here. Dictionaries only contain 'important' and 'public' words; thus words that describe alternatives to 'important' and 'public' ideas and institutions can either be left out or called 'slang'. The shared-intimacy meanings of 'getting off' or 'getting together' are unlikely to be found in most dictionaries, for instance, while the universal yet frowned upon 'fuck' has only very recently found its way into real dictionaries.

There is obviously a large element of embarrassment at work, too, since much of the reason why the words aren't acceptable is that people don't want to think about and talk about the things and ideas they describe, largely because those concepts are too threatening to their own world. Once the words have been left out of dictionaries, the language experts can tell us that the words don't exist or shouldn't be used. They can tell us that there are already perfectly good words to describe perfectly good models of relating, and thereby discourage the admission of new relating words to the ranks of dictionary-acceptable language.

These are some of the reasons why ideas about

normality and the power of the status quo keep the language of relating straitjacketed, but I think there are other reasons too, reasons more directly linked with the very nature of relating. Part of what makes things difficult is that the relationship or the behaviour that needs to be described is changing all the time, so all you can really describe is how things seem to you at present. Things often change so quickly that there seems little time to stop and put words to what is happening, and the changes are often too subtle to make linguistic distinctions. Any description, let alone any label, applied to a relationship will almost inevitably be incomplete.

Yet descriptions can help to clarify situations. If you have an agreement with somebody that for the time being you are going to have a monogamous relationship, then the use of the label 'monogamous' is accurate and useful, and almost certainly more useful than conventional labels like 'married' would be. Even though they can sometimes be useful, labels for relationships can also be very limiting, and if you really want to know something about the ways in which somebody conducts their relationships, you will have to go beyond labels to details that are normally considered private. I strongly believe that it's only by sharing our experience of hitherto 'private' behaviour that we can start to find out what we really need from our relationships, and in the process expand our vocabulary of useful words and concepts.

What we will almost certainly find as we explore ways of describing our relationships is that nearly all of the language we know and use already will not fit our experience precisely. Everything we say will need to be qualified: 'I am married but I have other friends who I am sometimes physically intimate with,' for example, or 'I think of myself as a lesbian but I have one or two very close men friends who I sometimes have cuddles with'. The need for qualification arises simply because words don't exist for a lot of the relationships we find ourselves in, and the descriptions we have – 'being married', 'going out together', 'living with', 'sleeping with' – just don't fit the facts of those relationships.

When honesty and clarity in relating are considered to be important, we need to be very aware of the limitations of the relationship language we have available to us, and where the language doesn't fit our experience we can experiment with different ways of describing our relationships until the words do fit the facts. It will probably seem contrived and longwinded, but I'm sure it's worth the effort. I appreciate it enormously if instead of introducing someone to me with: 'Well, we're sort of friends', you say something like: 'This is the person I share a flat with. We have our own rooms, and we're very close. Sometimes we share a bed, though we're not sexual.'

When we feel safe and confident enough to describe our relationships clearly, we will all know much better where we are. We shall have a sound basis for mutual trust and understanding, and limiting convention will have been dealt a body blow.

13

A Question of Violence

Sex and violence. Sex'n'violence. It isn't coincidental that they trip off the tongue so easily. As the numbed and numbing silence surrounding sexual violence – child abuse, rape, bullying, harassment, domestic violence – has begun to be broken, we see that it is little wonder that many of us find intimacy so frightening.

One child in five is thought to have been the victim of sexual abuse which, according to NSPCC figures, is thought to be rising at the rate of more than 20 per cent each year. Many cases involve supposedly 'responsible' and 'caring' adults: a 1990 police operation against a Liverpool 'child sex ring' involved company directors, an education authority official and several church ministers.

If child abuse is increasingly considered to be endemic in our culture, its incidence is still relatively low when compared with domestic violence against women. A 1989 survey by Hammersmith and Fulham Borough Council in London found that 48 per cent of women had been attacked or threatened by their partner in their home; 30 per cent had been assaulted; and 13 per cent had been threatened with being killed.

At some level I suspect that everybody has a deep fear and loathing of violence, especially when they can imagine it being wrought on themselves or on the people and things they love and are close to. People who allow themselves to feel their feelings will find it hard to be anything other than scared, sickened and saddened when they experience violent behaviour. Yet despite our fear of violent behaviour, we are nearly all, from an early age, spectators of seemingly endless violence. In our homes we switch on the radio or television, put on a video, or go to the pictures and suck sweeties, and take in the most horrific and terrible violence. It's a rare film, and an even rarer newscast, that doesn't include a single death or mutilation. Shooting, torture, burning, violent death and malicious damage are all part of most people's daily diet of media input.

The same media, backed up by popular wisdom, tell us that violence is a sort of modern epidemic, daily reaching greater proportions. Look at the news, look at the papers – bombings, kidnappings, rapes, murders. Even then we don't see it all. The popular emphasis on public mass violence plays down a lot of the violence experienced every day in every city, town and village. A forty-year-old woman beaten and burnt with a red-hot poker in her home in a village close to where I live doesn't make it to television and the national papers – it's not considered violent enough. After all, she was only in hospital for three days.

And what about the two young men I passed this morning carrying air rifles, or the child I overheard yesterday saying 'If you don't give it to me I'll punch your head in'? Some people would claim that these are nothing to do with violence, merely sport and childish teasing. But all this and much more is part of a celebration of violence, learned at a very early age, and then assumed to be simply the way the world is. Because it seems to be unrelated to public media violence, it's easy to pretend that it isn't violence at all. There is a general denial that violence takes place in happy families and nice neighbourhoods. Violence happens to other people in other places, on the other side of the television screen.

'Is man violent by nature?' asks Gerald Priestland in his book *The Future of Violence*, and his use of the word 'man' is certainly appropriate. Of course women break things, hurt and even kill people but, except in rare cases, women are less violent and are violent less often than men.

Crime statistics show this clearly. Nearly ten times as many men as women are found guilty of personal violence; over twelve times as many of criminal damage. In sexual offences including violence, men are nearly a hundred times more often prosecuted than women.

Some anthropologists, mostly male ones like Konrad Lorenz and Robert Ardrey, have studied aggression in depth. They have largely succeeded in convincing us that not only is aggression a natural and necessary part of human behaviour, but also that it is so pre-ordained by our biological make-up (those hormones are mostly to blame again) that we cannot help but be violent from time to time, especially if we're male. This excuse in relation to violence has become so much part of our cultural belief system that it's often very difficult to remember that violence is culturally learned, so even though it seems impossible, the same violence can be culturally refused. The 'I can't help it' line denies the creative intelligence and the ability to choose that are fundamental to our human nature. Even men have the potential to choose to react in radically different ways to threat and to injury.

In an article called 'Cherchez l'Homme' in her book *It's Only Me*, Jill Tweedie states bluntly and accurately that when male sociologists, philosophers and anthropologists talk about the problem of human aggression, what they really mean is the problem of male aggression. While these learned scholars look for the basic biological flaw in human anatomy to account for violence, they deliberately implicate women in what is clearly male behaviour. She goes on:

> And we women have believed them. But the truth is that most violence, most crime and most vice is not committed by human beings in general. It is committed by men.
>
> The creation, production, distribution and consumption of pornography is almost exclusively male. The motivation behind prostitution is male and the law that punishes prostitution is male-conceived and administered. Women do not take indecent photographs of nude children, women do not molest children. We talk of muggings and robbery with violence, of assault and grievous bodily harm as if such problems were endemic to the human race, but they are only endemic to one half of the race – the male half.
>
> We talk, euphemistically, of domestic violence, but which sex is domestically violent? Men. We talk of violence in the streets, but who is violent in the streets? Men. Hit-and-run drivers are mostly men, incest is almost exclusively instigated by men, wars are started and fought by men.
>
> A month ago, I monitored a fortnight's newspapers for reports of violence and vandalism. In every case, the felon was a man. Worse, in a disproportionate amount of cases, the victim was a woman.

Anger and aggression are often lumped together indiscriminately, but there are very important differences between the two, and distinguishing between them is not just playing with words. Anger is a feeling, a physical feeling associated with a tightening of the muscles, tension throughout the body, and increased mental activity. Aggression or violence certainly follows an angry feeling in many cases, but, unlike anger, aggression is an act, a form of behaviour.

The distinction between feeling and action is vital to any understanding of what can be done about violence, but the cultural link between anger and violence is very strong. The realisation that they can be separated, that the anger can be dealt with and the violence replaced, takes a great deal of experience and faith to recognise and implement.

What can be done with anger other than expressing it in violence? To begin with it's interesting to look at what people who are not generally violent do with their anger. Babies and young children scream when they're angry, and hit out with their arms and legs; they deal with the feelings immediately. For many people, and especially for women, unexpressed angry feelings and the tension that goes with them get locked up inside the body, causing physical stiffness and psychological and mental depression. Depression, often subtitled 'moodiness' or 'emotionality' and attached to women with distinctly negative connotations, is often believed to be as intrinsic to female nature as aggression is to men, and it's not surprising that in a world where what men do is considered to be the norm, the link between anger and depression is far less acknowledged than that between anger and violence.

Learning how to deal with anger means becoming aware of the double messages we receive and have received about anger, and becoming clear that we can choose how we deal with anger and violence. How many times have we been told not to get angry, how anger isn't good, how nice people don't get angry? But anger is a very healthy emotion, especially when we experience injustice, pain and violence. It would be a very unhealthy person who didn't feel anger if they came upon a man assaulting a child, or if they were unfairly criticised or made to stop doing something they had every right to do.

The anger then needs to be channelled into appropriate action, and this is where choice is important, especially as this is also where our upbringing and culture have often taught us totally inappropriate reactions. The anger and fear that a woman experiences when threatened by a man frequently expresses itself in physical rigidity accompanied by a scream, a reaction that both the woman and the man have been trained to expect. With the understanding that even in extreme situations you have a choice of reaction, it is clear that the advice given to women in self-defence training is both more appropriate and more effective: start running suddenly and shout for help.

In the chapter about homosexuality I talked about some of the ways in which men learn that the whole range of feelings – whether sadness, fear, joy, excitement or anger (as distinct from violence) – is considered to be weak and 'feminine'. It's not that men don't have feelings, it's that they're not expected to show them and thus have to pretend that they don't have them, especially to other men. Many men have spent so long pretending not to have feelings that they've managed to convince themselves that their feelings aren't real, thus making themselves into real men. While women are generally allowed to feel their feelings, the exception is anger. Anger is definitely not 'ladylike', though women have a great deal to be angry about.

The result of the denial of men's feelings is that, as we have seen, violence becomes the only culturally accepted way for men to express their feelings. Violence becomes the solution to any painful emotion, and frequently the only solution to joyful emotions too, as witness the damage that football supporters can wreak when their team wins. The alternatives, especially crying and screaming, are definitely out. A real man keeps his cool, he's tough, he never fails, and he never walks away from a fight.

Men have learnt this since they were very young. Even if they knew that violence wasn't the only answer, even if they had wanted things to be different, it's very difficult to go against the peer pressure and refuse to take part in the chasing, hitting, teasing and bullying that goes on in most school playgrounds, and is mostly instituted by boys. Judith Arcana listened to her six-year-old son Daniel describing his school playtime; how the boys chase the girls, knock them down and push them around and say they're going to look at their underpants; how if he doesn't run with the boys, they'll turn against him and attack him. 'What can this little boy do?' she asks in *Every Mother's Son*.

> What to make of the sharp understanding that the girls are the accepted prey of the boys, and that any boy who won't take his place in the pack is attacked, and vilified with the worst insult these male children have learned in their six years: he's called a *girl* – and treated as girls are treated. Given the choice Daniel was given, how many small boys, even the most gentle and non-sexist, would have chosen to martyr themselves, to become one of the despised ones?

The initiation of boys into violence is frequently quite a structured process, well described by Anne-Marie Fearon in the feminist magazine *Shrew*:

> You frighten children with a monster mask or a cap-gun. In the case of a girl you don't let her retaliate, tell her that girls don't put on ugly faces or play with guns, let her feel frightened, cry, and run to mother. Boys are forbidden to cry or run to mother (if he does he's called a wet or a drip), and

you teach him to deny his hurt and fear. This is very hard and puts him under constant tension, so you give him a gun and a monster mask, and now whenever he feels that tension he can channel it into aggression and project his fears on to someone else. He's now ready to frighten the next generation of little ones, and so keep the whole system going.

Without consciously choosing alternative outlets for anger, violence continues to be the all-too-usual way for men as they grow up to show that they have any strong feelings at all. But the alternatives do exist, are well established, and work. The practical details of dealing with anger depend very much on the individual person and how they feel and express their anger. The different methods would take too much space to talk about here, but there are some good guides, among which are *Learning to Live Without Violence*, a book for men by Daniel Sonkin and Michael Durphy, and *The Feeling Good Book* by Louis Proto. Most of the techniques involve separating anger and violence, being able to recognise the early signs of anger, taking the anger to a safe place away from its apparent source so you can shout and hit things without hurting or destroying anyone or anything, and giving yourself enough time to feel what the anger is about and to recover from it.

Because women are generally not allowed to show their feelings of anger at all, and certainly not in a violent way, a different approach to anger is often needed, one that concentrates on being able to experience and communicate anger rather than on being able to rechannel anger away from violence. Anne Dickson, in *A Woman in Your Own Right*, describes how an angry woman will often grit her teeth, swallow back and cry rather than get angry, ending up feeling frustrated and depressed. Chapter 10 of her excellent book describes in detail how to feel and communicate anger in a clear and creative way, and contains many good suggestions which are useful both for women and for men.

The incidence of violence, and particularly of domestic violence, is tied in with many other beliefs about family and sexuality, some of which have already been discussed in earlier chapters. If a man believes that he owns his wife and his children, he can also believe that he can do what he wants with them. Such 'minor' incidents as hitting your children or slapping your wife's face are too often accepted by society as just part of the way the world is.

The privacy of the family allows much violence to continue without being observed, and if the knowledge of that violence seeps out of the home it usually meets a very mixed response. It is becoming increasingly clear that most incidents of wife-battering and child abuse are not reported, and this is particularly true where supposedly 'lesser' violences are perpetrated which cannot be proved from scars and injuries. Nobody except the people involved know the fear and pain of what's going on, partly because loyalty to the family is accorded so much importance, partly because of the stigma attached to admitting that all is far from well in your 'happy family', and partly because the chances are that few people will believe you and even fewer will support you.

In her book about incest, *Conspiracy of Silence*, Sandra Butler tells the true story of a woman, Margaret, who discovered that her oldest child, a girl then five years old, was being sexually molested by her husband. Over the next ten years Margaret was aware that her other three children were being assaulted, yet everyone around her, from her sister-in-law to the officials at the campsite where her fourteen-year-old son was raped, told her that 'these things go on all the time', that it was 'only natural' and 'no big thing', so not to get worked up about it.

212 & Getting Closer

Teachers at the children's school said they would only intervene if the children requested it, which they never did, and the local police chief's advice was to 'get a gun and blow the bastard away if he ever comes close to your kids again'. When in desperation she took her problem to the church she had attended for many years, their reaction was to recommend unanimously that she should attend no more church functions until she had things 'straightened out at home'.

In this way violence within the family is simultaneously silenced and accepted, denied and condoned. But it is not only oppressive beliefs about the family that sanction domestic violence; many of our cultural beliefs about sexuality also provide apparent grounds for aggression at home and elsewhere. As I said at the start of this chapter, the link between sex and violence has entered popular mythology as an inextricable 'sex'n'violence' category for a wide range of fantasy, both written and visual. Much of the language of male-fantasy sex and male-fantasy war is identical – talk of conquest, of winning, of rape, force and capture.

Violence in the field of sex has expert approval. The knowledgeable *Visual Dictionary of Sex* (Medical Editor-in-Chief Doctor Eric J. Trimmer), alongside a picture of a half-naked and bound woman, screaming while she has one breast squeezed hard and the other beaten with a cane, says: 'Practically everyone gets a kick out of giving pain. Most of it is an expression of a built-in desire to be cruel and powerful. People like reading about sadism, so it is understandable that they get pleasure from a little harmless expression of sadism in their sex-play. A back deeply scratched in passionate frenzy is a minor example.' The section on 'Erotic Bondage' is even more appalling: 'Using body piercing, rings can be attached to the nipples, the foreskin, the vaginal lips and so on. Sometimes the woman is gagged with a mask that resembles the medieval "scold's bridle‹, thus satisfying a common male desire to silence and punish the woman who knows how to wound his ego with words.'

I simply do not believe that freely chosen violence within sexual behaviour is part of most people's personal experience. I've talked with many people about intimacy and sexuality, and not once has anybody told me about a first-hand experience of *voluntarily chosen* pain and violence during a sexual encounter. I'm not saying it doesn't happen, simply that the deliberate introduction of pain into sexual sharing with the active agreement of both partners is a rare phenomenon. People – nearly always women – have often talked about violence that has been done to them, but the idea that sexual partners mutually choose extreme forms of pain and humiliation as part of their enjoyment of sex remains almost exclusively within the fantasies of sex manuals and pornographic magazines and films.

It's a short step from 'woman as possession' and 'sex as sadistic conquest' to the twisted logic of rape – a paradoxical act, repulsive to nearly everyone, yet holding an aura of fascination that the media finds difficult to resist. It's yet another manifestation of 'culturally acceptable' violence for many men, who refuse to imagine a woman's experience of feeling unsafe in her own world. It makes things worse to know that while the extremes of sexual assault are being celebrated by the media, the majority of assault incidents are considered too trivial to warrant attention, never mind the vast number of times when a woman is coerced into participating in a sexual encounter against her will. No wonder most women are fearful of encounters with dubious men, and are more suspicious than they would like to be – they have very good reason to be.

Because of the power men exert over women – physical power, the power to leave a woman looking after children with no money, the power to win court cases – women are put in an impossible double bind when deciding how to respond to a man. If a woman does accept lifts from men, does accept a cup of coffee, does wear fewer clothes, then she's considered 'easy prey'. It's claimed that she 'asked for it', especially if the court can prove that she's 'sexually experienced'. If she 'solicits a man' (we'll come back to those words soon) and is assaulted, or even murdered, popular opinion is unlikely to be sympathetic. If, on the other hand, she is so careful that she never puts herself 'at risk' – never spends time alone with men, never accepts a lift, never lets a man into her home – not only might she be depriving herself of enjoyable company, but she will probably be considered to be neurotic and mentally disturbed. But as long as rape is condoned, which is as long as men see violence as an acceptable way of relating to women, the assault will continue, and women's fears will be entirely rational.

One male myth that provides a perverted logic for rape and prostitution is that men have to get their sex somewhere, and if they can't find women willing to give it to them (and only women can give it to them), they either have to take it by force or pay for it. You don't have to be much of a logician to see that this argument hinges on a host of oppressive assumptions – that men have uncontrollable sexual needs, that sex is an exchangeable commodity, that women provide sex for men, that men have the money to buy what they need. Because women have 'the product' and men the cash, popular opinion has it that prostitutes 'solicit' business and money from their clients. It's certainly true that prostitutes need the money they earn, but it's the men who do the soliciting, as anyone who has watched what happens on the streets of a red light district at night knows only too well.

Sexual assault doesn't only happen in the home and on the streets. Since the early 1970s, sexual harassment in a woman's place of work has been named and become part of our conscious experience. As with domestic violence and rape, harassment at work is difficult to deal with because at the same time its existence is denied by many people and yet is actively supported by many men. It not only exists; sexual harassment at work is extremely common. A series of surveys discussed by Sue Read in her *Sexual Harassment at Work* shows that between 70 and 80 per cent of American and half of British working women have experienced uninvited sexual attention at work. In the area of work, where women are already so disadvantaged, these figures are horrific, especially when the refusal of the woman to participate in the enforced sexual exchange so often leads to retaliation and dismissal.

Not only is violence unnecessary and destructive, it's also well established that aggression is biologically poisonous and addictive. Any sort of stressful situation, including emotional trauma and physical pain, stimulates the adrenal glands to produce adrenalin, the purpose of which is to prepare the body for extreme activity by stimulating breathing and raising blood pressure and pulse rate. Desmond Morris and his determinist colleagues have apparently sanctioned violence by saying that there is a biological need to expend this physical energy in aggression. This is dangerous nonsense; the energy can just as easily be expended in shouting, stamping your feet, hitting a cushion, dancing, or singing at the top of your voice.

You can even postpone the letting out of the energy, the using up of the adrenalin high, until it feels safe to shout and hit, but what you can't do is expect large amounts of adrenalin simply to go away.

Many people believe they cannot live without a diet of trauma and violence, their dependence being very similar to a drug addiction. Part of learning to be a real man is learning to harden yourself against violence, not jumping when the gun goes off, laughing when people are killed. The result is that the artificial state of tension thus created by continuously high stress levels comes to be considered as quite normal. For these people, peace and calm are abnormal and frightening, and are conveniently thought of as cissy.

Armed (oops – it's so pervasive) with some understanding of the nature of violence, where do we go from here in our efforts to change things?

❀ We can recognise the difference between the necessary and important emotion of anger and the destructive and senseless action of aggression.

❀ We can make space for the safe expression of pain and trauma, and encourage and allow people to feel their fear and anger.

❀ We can help children, especially little boys, not to be frightened into violence. We can rescue them from scary experiences and let them know that it is good and important for them to feel their feelings.

❀ We can recognise the phenomenon of addiction to violence, and rescue ourselves from it by turning the television off or putting the book down when we start to feel the effects of stress addiction. We can stop scaring ourselves.

❀ We can explore alternative ways of hanging on to our personal power without needing to resort to violence; this is the practice of non-violent action.

❀ We can work on ways of resolving differences of opinion using understanding and compassion rather than aggression and competition.

❀ We can help to provide easily approachable channels for people for whom violence is a problem they want to deal with: refuges for battered women; support groups for the victims of violence; groups for men who want to deal with their violent behaviour, such as the Domestic Violence Diversion programmes in the United States.

✾ We can refuse to accept that violence is a 'natural' outlet of feelings, or that violence is ever the solution to a problem.

The last thing to be done about violence, and probably the most important, I leave to a woman to state clearly and unequivocally. In an essay called 'Redefining Non-violence' (reprinted in *Our Blood*), the American feminist Andrea Dworkin speaks primarily to women, but her words are for everybody to hear and act on:

> As women, non-violence must begin for us in the refusal to be violated, in the refusal to be victimised. We must find alternatives to submission, because our submission perpetuates violence. The refusal to be a victim does not originate in any act of resistance as male-derived as killing. The refusal of which I speak is a revolutionary refusal to be a victim, any time, any place, for friend or foe. Male aggression feeds on female masochism as vultures feed on carrion. Our nonviolent project is to find the social, sexual, political and cultural forms which repudiate our programmed submissive behaviours, so that male aggression can find no dead flesh on which to feast.

14

Dirty Pictures, Filthy Lies

Everybody knows what pornography is, or at least everyone who feels strongly about it does. The men who stand in sex shops leafing through the glossy magazines know very well that what they're looking at is pornography. Anita Bryant, Mary Whitehouse, and the Festival of Light know that what they're fighting against is pornography. And when feminists like Andrea Dworkin and Susan Griffin write books about pornography they certainly know what they mean by the word. Although the material in question – the books, photographs, films and videos – is often, though not always, identical, each group's definition of pornography will be very different, and each will have experts and dictionaries to back them up. The reason for this is that all of them want to maintain the correctness of their version, since it represents things so central to their different views of the nature of human relationships.

My primary reason for including a chapter about pornography in a book about close relationships is that, whatever definition of pornography is being used, a great deal of our culture's approach to intimacy is centred around – and set in focus by – the images of sexuality presented by the more risqué (or smutty, depending on your outlook) of the popular media. Britain's largest-selling newspaper, *The Sun*, each day carries a photograph of a near-naked woman. Advertising and the film industry thrive on sexual titillation. More than two million men regularly buy magazines like *Men Only*, *Knave* and *Mayfair*, and the pornography industry in Britain has an estimated turnover of more than a billion pounds a year.

Whether we like it or not, pornography – whoever's definition we use – plays a central role in the sexual education and sexual culture of contemporary Britain. Whether this is acceptable or not, dangerous or not, evil or not, depends a great deal upon our experience of and reaction to pornographic material. This in turn depends upon how we define the word. It's usually not the elements of pornography that are in question, but the interpretations of what those elements represent. Let's look at these constituents and see what the basic disagreements are about.

With the exception of a small amount of material produced for gay men, the primary subject of almost all pornography is women. Where men are depicted it is usually as the possessors and masters of women. The women in pornography are not just any women; they are displayed women, anonymous women, available for anybody who has enough money – a couple of pounds each for *Playboy* and *Mayfair*, about twenty pence a woman. The public availability of anonymous women's bodies is nothing new – in ancient Greece the lowest class of prostitute, with a status even lower than that of the lowest slave, was called *porne*, giving us the literal meaning of pornography, the definition of the *Oxford English Dictionary*: 'a depiction of the life, manners, etc. of prostitutes and their patrons'. Nobody denies that pornography almost exclusively depicts women; the difference is that while the purveyors of pornography try to persuade us that pornography represents women as they really are, those who find pornography oppressive and degrading, including most women, believe otherwise. They believe that pornography not only fails entirely to represent the reality of being a woman, but also that the vast bulk of pornography's portrayal of women is the product of the pornographer's warped imagination, and has no link whatsoever with the experience of real human beings.

Another element of pornography is nudity – hence 'skinflicks' and 'striptease'. Again, pornographers claim to show naked bodies and nudity as they really are; the opponents of pornography see this as a further excuse for pornographers to resort to lies and fantasies about the human body, and especially about women's bodies.

It's not just any part of the body that wins attention in the pornographic image – the sexual parts and what they do and what is done to them are central to pornography. The American *Merriam-Webster Dictionary* makes sex central to its definition of pornography: 'The depiction of erotic behaviour designed primarily to cause sexual excitement.' Morse Peckham, in his *Art and Pornography*, is even more specific: 'Pornography is the presentation in verbal or visual signs of human sexual organs in a condition of stimulation.' Pornography claims to tell truths about sexuality, and particularly about women's sexuality. Opponents of pornography believe that it lies perniciously about sexuality, and particularly about women's sexuality.

An important element in pornography, especially in film and video, is the portrayal of force and violence as part of sexual behaviour. 'But we only show the world as it is,' say the pornographers. 'Violence is part of the way things are, men are naturally aggressive in sex', and 'There is a certain masochistic streak in many women: they occasionally desire to be overpowered and treated a little roughly'. Opponents of pornography believe that this is nonsense. They believe that pornography helps to maintain force and aggression as legitimate means for men to take power over women, particularly for sexual gratification.

In *The Joy of Sex*, Alex Comfort defines pornography as 'any sexual literature that somebody is trying to repress', certainly one interesting definition of pornography. Every aspect of sexuality, whether feelings, physical activity or social behaviour, has somebody who is trying to repress it, which by Alex Comfort's definition would make any material that deals with sexuality pornographic. Pornographers generally try to repress at least as many aspects of sexuality as anybody else; they choose to discount tenderness and affection. Thus this becomes a very confused definition to use unless you also make clear *what* is being repressed and *who* is doing the repressing.

Pornographers often like to portray themselves as front-line fighters in the battle for personal freedom and individual rights. But the freedom they are fighting for is the freedom for men to maintain an oppressive view of the world which depends entirely on the subjugation of women and children, and where sexual behaviour is reduced to a few stereotyped activities. Pornographers object to the suppression of material mostly depicting naked women involved in sexual behaviour, often involving violence. They caricature the opposition as a narrow-minded spoilsport section of the population (mostly neurotic women) who don't want to let libertarian free-thinking people indulge in perfectly harmless activities.

On the other hand, most opponents of pornography find pornography disturbing, disgusting and degrading: anti-love and anti-sexuality. They see pornographers taking advantage of and exaggerating already warped ideas about sexuality and violence, especially in relation to women. But here the opponents of pornography divide. Not surprisingly the pornographers are ever willing to expose and take advantage of the division to their own ends.

On one side of the divide are people who object to pornography on the grounds that it erodes the traditional values of womanhood, family and married sexuality. What they want to suppress is almost any change from long-standing tradition regarding sexuality and intimate relating. Thus the Festival of Light, and more specifically its founder, Mary Whitehouse, would like to see an end to any mention of sexuality on television, to the public use of 'bad language', and to the publication of anything that questions traditional sexual roles and values. I don't think she'd be at all happy about this book.

Many other people, including feminist women and their allies, object to pornography on the grounds that it is an important and extreme element of a male-defined culture based on the denial of women as equal and important human beings, depicting them instead as impersonal and dispensable objects. What these people would like to suppress is material that presents such a view of the world, but, unlike the traditional moralists, they are well aware that suppression of material without questioning the assumptions behind pornography does little to change the prevalence and status of pornography. Legislating against pornography simply entrenches self-styled libertarians against their opponents, and while legal definitions of pornography remain as they are, much important material which questions accepted views of women, sex and relating will fall foul of the same legislation that supposedly controls the wares of the pornographers. As Ruth Wallsgrove writes in an article entitled 'Pornography: Between the Devil and the True Blue Whitehouse', 'Censorship laws are always used against those who attempt to inform women about the basics of their reproductive organs, let alone their sexuality, while backstreet blue movies always find a way to survive.'

Common to all pornographic material is the fact that, almost without exception, it is produced by men and for men. Pornographers claim otherwise: many spirited defences of pornography include phrases like 'People should have the right to read what they want to'. Only the definition of pornography as 'writing about prostitutes' comes near to acknowledging the universally known truth that where pornography is concerned, 'people' doesn't mean everybody, it means men. Pornography is financed by men, engineered by men, marketed by men and consumed by men. 'What about the women shown in pornography?' ask the liberal-minded supporters of a right of access to pornography, 'Don't they have a choice as to whether they involve themselves in the production of pornography? Don't they enjoy doing it really?' To begin with this ignores the economic pull of earning money from a source that never seems to dry up, especially for women relating to men who are involved in pornography. It also ignores the possible coercion of women by men into activities they don't want to be involved in, and the threats that women face if they decide not to co-operate. And far from loving every moment, here is blue movie actress Georgia Stark, quoted in the magazine *Newsweek*: 'The first film I made was really a downer. Afterwards I started to think about suicide. But after a while I got so I could do the Eleanor Rigby thing – you know, leave your mind in a jar by the door. Then I'd know I'm just an animal and they are taking pictures of an animal.'

Adding all these elements together, we arrive at an overview of pornography as the depiction of women, undressed or undressing, obviously sexual, and often being forced or done violence to. Pornographic material is often in danger of being suppressed, and it's produced and consumed in a male-defined and male-dominated setting. If we go back to the original meaning of pornography, especially in Andrea Dworkin's interpretation of the definition as 'writing about whores', it's clear that this exactly describes the perceived nature of the bulk of pornography, and the assumptions that lie behind it.

In so many ways the assumptions underlying the pornographic view of the world are exactly the same as those I have already questioned when looking at sexuality, relationships and violence. They include the belief that men own women; the belief that women exist largely to service men; the belief that women's sexuality is defined by their relationship to men; and the belief that violence is innate to human nature. Since these assumptions are fundamental to the pornographic view of the world, it's impossible to support pornography without supporting lies, exploitation, oppression and violence. Put even more simply, there is little if no distinction: pornography is lies, pornography is exploitation, pornography is oppression, and pornography is violence.

Another common claim made by pornographers and their supporters is that pornography represents some sort of truth about human behaviour, and that it therefore has an educational role in teaching people how to relate. Some clinics and doctors claim that showing men the possibilities of sexual behaviour portrayed in pornographic magazines can 'cure' sexual 'dysfunctions'. Sheila Kitzinger, in *Women's Experience of Sex*, describes how one doctor shows pictures of a naked woman being tied up and beaten, supposedly to cure impotence. The 'educational' role of pornography has a long history: on 9 February 1668 Samuel Pepys confessed to his diary that 'I did read through *The School of Maidens*, a lewd book, but what doth me no wrong to read for information sake.'

A cursory glance at even so-called 'soft' pornography shows that the portrayal of women in the pornographic fantasy world is very far removed from the everyday experience both of the women it purports to portray and of the men who buy it. When did you last see a fierce-looking brunette woman on a beach wearing half a diving suit, her bottom in the air and her legs wide open? Or a blonde woman with a come-hither look, lying on a sofa in a garden, wearing nothing but a basque around her waist, and again with her legs wide apart? Or a secretary wearing only a suspender belt and high heels, crouching on hands and knees, nipples erect even though the temperature of the room is high enough to keep her goose pimples at bay, with the telephone cord neatly inserted between her labia? Unless you inhabit a very different world from most people, I would be very surprised indeed if scenes like this were part of your daily experience, yet this is the fantasy view of the world purveyed regularly by the 'men's magazines' – in this case in a recent issue of *Knave*.

It's not at all that fantasy is bad or unimportant, but what distinguishes pornographic fantasy from creative fantasy is its claim to represent some degree of reality about women and their relationship to men. The publishers of magazines like *Knave* and *Penthouse* may claim that their customers understand that the stories and images in pornographic magazines and books represent a fantasy version of reality, but the truth is that they deliberately portray pornography in settings with which men can readily identify. *Mayfair*'s 'Quest' pages ('The laboratory of human response'), for example, bring pornographic fantasy home to roost in Swansea, Banbury and Edinburgh, while the *Men Only* classifieds offer visiting masseusses, 'real housewives' naughties', and 'warm moist underwear'.

I think that many lonely, frustrated men are taken in by the carrot held out to them by the pornographers – and subsequently despise themselves for it. And they keep coming back for more, even though they know full well that they will be disappointed. 'Tragic and joyless' is how

Lynne Segal describes it in her book about men, *Slow Motion*, and quotes feminist Deirdre English's 1980 description of a visit to New York's notorious Times Square: 'The men are here to exploit the women; the women are here to exploit the men. The overwhelming feeling is of the exploitation of male sexual desire. There it is, embarrassingly desperate, tormented, demeaning itself, begging for relief, taking any substitute and *paying* for it. Men who live for this are suckers, and their uncomfortable demeanour shows they know it.'

As with violence, the confusion between fantasy and reality often makes the distinction between the two an almost impossible task. It's made particularly difficult for men, who often have no alternative model presented to them than the world of male fantasy. Their need to believe in the fantasy, together with the inability to express sensitivity that comes from an education in macho hardness, creates a craving for ever more grotesque sensation, which pornographers are always willing to accommodate. When soft pornography fails, harder drugs are available, and the fantasies increasingly lose touch with reality.

The trouble is that the producers and consumers of pornography (particularly the latter; I think the producers know *exactly* what they're doing) find it more and more difficult to tell the difference. Trauma and horror lose all meaning; sensitivity doesn't get a look-in. Nudity isn't enough, but it's difficult to take off more than your clothes; dying isn't enough, people should die as slowly and nastily as possible.

The availability of pornography is often justified on the grounds that people should be free to do whatever they want with their own lives, which ties in with the definition of pornography as something that is suppressed. The equation of pornography with personal freedom fails on two counts. First, a person can only do what they want with their own life if they are willing to be totally selfish, even when other people are hurt and degraded in the process. Secondly, as we have already seen, the freedom of access to pornography can only be the freedom of access to an oppressive and degrading view of women, their sexuality and their emotions. The freedom to oppress other people, which is the sort of freedom being requested by the supporters of pornography, is entirely different from the individual freedom to express your own power and beauty, sensitively and responsibly.

It's time now to look at some of the things that pornography may be confused with. While it's true that the borders of pornography are often hard to define, it's also important to acknowledge that men who produce and sell pornography also want to keep the definition of pornography as vague as possible, thus persuading their customers to consume their wares whether they are actually pornographic or not. The same confusion about boundaries works in the other direction too – to call something pornographic when it isn't with the aim of suppressing it is using the vagueness of definition to oppressive ends just as surely as the pornographers do.

One boundary that people have great problems with is the one between pornography and art. The problems arise partly because both terms are kept deliberately vague, and partly because both terms are not so much a description of a certain sort of material as a way of making that material acceptable to a particular audience. If you own a porn shop, you want your customers to believe that what you have in your shop is pornography; if you're a fine art dealer you need to convince your customers that what you have on display is art. Trying to make any other distinction between pornography and art is almost certain to fail, because there are no objective standards. Where a book or picture portrays some of the standard elements of pornography, it can often be classified equally easily under either heading. You'll find Henry Miller and Norman Mailer in high-class bookshops as well as porn shops; paintings by Courbet, Dali and Magritte which hang in art galleries illustrate pornshop erotica. There's nothing to prevent words and pictures being art and pornography at the same time and, as John Berger makes clear in his book *Ways of Seeing*, the stereotypes, especially of women, are displayed very similarly in art gallery catalogues and 'girlie' magazines.

Two particular art forms almost invariably fall into this debatable middle ground. In the way they are usually represented, both 'the nude' and 'erotica' are more or less pornographic, though there is no fundamental reason why they should be. The nude in art galleries is justified in terms of beauty, form and composition or, rather daringly, in terms of sensuality or eroticism. Since art gallery nudes are 'art', it would not be considered at all nice to admit to finding them sexually, or even emotionally, stimulating. Yet whatever its justification in painting, sculpture and photography, it doesn't take much experience of observing 'the nude' to realise that it isn't usually just anybody without their clothes on. The nude is usually young, attractive (by the standards of the culture in which it was created) and female – exactly the same qualities that men look for in pornographic models and prostitutes. Here is the old double standard at work again: the nude is supposed to celebrate the beauty of the human form, but only certain sorts of bodies are acceptable. 'The nude' is mostly about stereotypically attractive women without clothes on for men to look at, and as such cannot be far from pornographic. Art gallery nudes and books on nude photography usually tell you as little as men's magazines do about the way ordinary people look without their clothes on.

The same is true of erotica, a term that has come to mean something which describes or illustrates sexual behaviour. As with the nude, if erotica really did represent the range of human sensual experience in a loving and sensitive way, it would have an important part to play in learning about and exploring physical closeness. But most 'erotica' is not about the variety of intimacy; it's about men pressing their sexual fantasies on less-than-willing women, and it's created by men for men. The fact that it comes from another country or from an earlier age, or that it is found in big coffee-table books rather than pornographic magazines, is no let-out. Pornography has existed for a long time; putting pictures of ancient oriental oppressive sexual practices between hard glossy covers and calling it erotica makes it no less pornographic.

No amount of calling pornography something else will make it less pornographic. A picture or a book may be any or all of artistic, erotic, realistic and informative, but if it also exploits and degrades, celebrates sexual violence, and gives an oppressive male-fantasy view of the world, it is also pornographic.

At the same time, just because words and pictures describe women, relationships, nudity and sexuality, there is no reason at all why they should be pornographic. Because nudity and sexuality have become synonymous with pornography (why else does the naturist magazine *Health and Efficiency* share the newsagent's shelf with *Playboy* and *Mayfair*?) it is difficult to envisage books and pictures dealing with these subjects which are not pornographic. Pornography is often advertised as being explicit, a description that means 'clear, precise, developed in detail', but who needs clear and precise information about the pornographers' version of interpersonal relating? Being explicit about intimacy and sexuality is crucial to understanding ourselves and our relationships. It's not the qualities of precision and clarity that need to be altered, it's the reality being portrayed. It's not the explicit depiction of nudity or sexuality that needs to be suppressed – far from it. Will McBride's book of photographs for children called *Show Me*, and Nancy Durrell McKenna's photographs for Sheila Kitzinger's *Woman's Experience of Sex*, show intimacy and sexuality as an integral part of warm and compassionate relating. The photographs by Sjan Bijman and Bertien van Manen for Anja Meulenbelt's *For Ourselves*, or Anne Severson's film of women's genitals called *Chakra*, are both very explicit about women's sexuality, yet because they allow women to be themselves rather than distorted by men's fantasies, because they do not mention, far less glorify, violence, and because they are not intended primarily for male consumption, they are clearly not pornographic.

But the law insists on defining pornography by virtue of its degree of explicitness, ignoring both its oppressive nature and its original meaning, and censorship laws can thus be used to prohibit material that can do a lot to help people understand the beauty and power of their bodies and emotions. When in 1977 the feminist magazine *Spare Rib* published a description of how women could check their breasts for potentially malignant lumps, it was considered obscene in Ireland and banned. Early in 1983 Will McBride's *Show Me* was declared obscene in the United States, because it shows naked people enjoying their bodies; no British publisher has yet dared to publish it. In March 1991 customs officials seized a number of erotic lesbian videos produced by the American women's group Fatale, which had been ordered by the British feminist writer Jenny White.

The producers and supporters of pornography can attempt to justify their wares until the cows come home, but true freedom and the full appreciation of the joy and variety of human relating can only exist in a world that can celebrate intimacy and sexuality without the need for pornography. At the end of her book called *Pornography:*

Men Possessing Women, Andrea Dworkin affirms her belief in such a world: 'The boys are betting that their penises and fists and knives and fucks and rapes will turn us into what they say we are – the compliant women of sex, the voracious cunts of pornography, the masochistic sluts who resist because we really want more. The boys are betting. The boys are wrong.'

The boys who believe that pornography justifies its existence are wrong, but so are those people who want to suppress material that explores the potential of loving and compassionate intimacy, and here there are exciting possibilities for replacing the pornographic view of physical closeness and sexuality with books and pictures which describe the humane, compassionate alternatives boldly and explicitly. The obstacles to producing such material appear overwhelming – the iron grip of pornographic fantasy, the censorship laws, the dangers of having motives and images distorted to fit the prevalent oppression of which pornography is a part.

But pornography cannot continue to be the only model of intimacy and sexuality available to generations of growing children. They need images of positive, powerful and loving closeness, and as yet very few such books and films exist. The current consumers of pornography may seem beyond the pale to the opponents of pornography, but given an opportunity to look at and read about loving and compassionate – and explicit – intimacy which portrays the variety of non-oppressive human relating, I believe that most men would be enormously relieved to have an alternative to the monotony and disappointment of pornography. And women, with the chance to enjoy their physical power and beauty without needing the approval of men and male standards, need to be reassured that bodies and sexuality exist to be enjoyed in as many different ways as their owners desire.

Joanna Russ puts the argument brilliantly in her essay

collection *Magic Mommas, Trembling Sisters, Puritans and Perverts*. 'The best cure for pornography is sex,' she writes, 'by which I mean autonomously chosen activity, freely engaged in for the sake of real pleasure, intense, and unmistakably the real thing. The more we have experiences like this, the less we will be taken in by the confusions and lies and messes all around us.'

15

Women, Men, and the Freedom to Be

I said at the start of this book that confusion seems to be the keyword of intimate relating in the 1990s. Many (of those of us old enough to have experienced it) had their outlook on life radically changed by the sexual revolution of the 1960s; even more were touched by the ideas and demands of the women's movement which grew and flourished during the 1970s. Nobody who has lived through the Thatcher years can have been unaffected by the cultural individualism and moral retrenchment of the 1980s.

Each of these phases in the questioning of conventional values has resulted in important insights and radical shifts in the way we behave. Yet such rapidly changing values – almost fashions in relating – have left many people frustrated and uncertain, both about what they really want from the people closest to them and about how to achieve it. The result is that most people have a more or less constant sense of dissatisfaction with the way they relate (or don't relate) intimately. Shere Hite's massive survey on *Women and Love*, for example, suggests that 98 per cent of the women she questioned wanted fundamental changes in their relationships with men.

As we have seen, much of this dissatisfaction arises because very few people are addressing the fundamental question of what it is that people really need in close relationships. If you don't know what you need, it's highly unlikely that you'll get it – or that you'll recognise it if and when it comes your way. Yet instead of looking carefully at what constitutes a human being's most basic emotional needs, we have become caught up in an economy in which all the elements of supposedly successful relating – from romantic novels to sex aids – are set out on the counter to be bought like painkillers and frozen peas. Ours has become a world of things rather than feelings; possessions rather than rights; separateness rather than relationship. Largely as a result of this concentration on materialism, consumption and competition, it is also a world in crisis, on the brink of dramatic and potentially cataclysmic change.

Yet alongside the violence and destruction, pollution and oppression – to a large extent in direct response to it – the last thirty years have seen an unprecedented grass-roots demand for radical social and political change. The overthrow of white supremacy in South Africa and the demise of state communism in the former Soviet bloc are but the most obvious signs that people will not for ever accept oppression as the status quo. All over the world there are indications that the seeds of sensitivity and freedom that were sown during the 1960s and 1970s are now bearing fruit as a more visionary generation (once branded as hippies, peaceniks and revolutionaries) begin to reach influential positions where their voices are being heard and taken note of.

Though men, being the more visible, have frequently taken the credit for the political and social reforms now forcing change in the global agenda, it is undoubtedly women who have done more than their share of planting and tending the seeds of social reform. This becomes very clear when we look at who it is that is pressing for changes at the level of the home and the community. Whether in the vanguard of nationwide tree-planting campaigns in Africa, or demanding an equal say in the workplace, women the world over are putting into practice the principle that 'the personal is political'.

This important insight, making it clear that our 'private' behaviour and experience is just as valid – and as open to questioning – as our public face, is just one of many radical yet commonsense statements emanating from the renaissance of feminism in the late twentieth century. Even if the recent major shifts in women's expectations are not readily acknowledged as being the result of the raising of feminist consciousness, it would be hard for anybody in the 1990s to ignore the existence of the women's movement.

The early growth of feminism in the nineteenth and early twentieth centuries is now well documented, though it is important to realise how much recent historical writing about and analysis of this period has resulted from the expanding consciousness of the women's movement, with its twin aims of understanding the historical precedents of contemporary feminism and redressing the balance of history which, until recently, was defined almost exclusively by men.

As women like Rebecca West and Dora Russell make clear in Dale Spender's book, *There's Always Been a Women's Movement This Century*, the spark of feminism was carried right through the period of 'traditional' values after the second world war. But in the late 1960s and early 1970s it was fanned into flames, largely as a result of such important books as Betty Friedan's *The Feminine Mystique*, Kate Millett's *Sexual Politics*, Germaine Greer's *The Female Eunuch* and Shulamith Firestone's *The Dialectic of Sex*. In the United States an important event was the adoption of a manifesto for women by the Women's Liberation Workshop in 1967, and a similar British Workshop started in 1969. The first of a series of British Women's Liberation Conferences was held in Oxford in February 1970, and International Women's Day in March 1971 brought thousands of women on to the streets of London to demonstrate and call for the first basic demands of the movement: equal pay; equal education and job opportunities; free contraception and abortion on demand; and free nurseries under community control. In 1974 two further demands were added: legal and financial independence; and an end to discrimination against lesbians and the right to a self-defined sexuality. A call in mid-1978 for freedom from sexual intimidation and male aggression brought the list of the movement's demands to seven.

By the early 1980s the movement had burgeoned and diversified, rather as the green movement is now broadening its focus. In much the same way as it is now being recognised that everything has environmental roots and implications, the 1980s saw the insights and understandings of feminism reaching into every sphere of human activity – from health, education and work to literature, art and drama.

The women's movement is neither a well-defined group nor a highly organised network. It includes many groups and individuals working on a wide range of social, political and economic issues. In common with other alternative movements, the women's movement has evolved ways of organising its activities that differ markedly from the methods of most other organisations. Theory, purpose and practice are closely interwoven, designed to serve the specific needs of the movement, needs that many women feel cannot be fulfilled using the organisational models presented within most of Western society.

Within the women's movement the importance of the individual person is recognised much more than in society at large. There are few leaders and official spokeswomen. Where a 'representative' organisation has tried to elevate itself to being *the* mouthpiece of the movement, as in France in the early 1980s, the reaction has been swift and angry.

This move towards anti-authoritarianism is far more than the need for a more representative democracy. It is a realisation that each person needs to be able to express their deepest feelings and insights in a supportive context, and not be judged for being the only thing they can be – socially patterned but nevertheless potentially happy, powerful people. It is an understanding that much of the anger, depression and confusion that so many people are feeling is an inevitable response to a society that systematically belittles personal power, individuality and creative expression, especially in women. And it is a recognition of the potential of women, when adequately encouraged and supported, to play a significant part in the changing of society's structures and attitudes.

One of the most important building blocks of the women's movement is the consciousness-raising group: women coming together to share, in a trusting and supportive setting, their personal experiences and insights. The importance of consciousness-raising cannot be overstressed; until problems and ways of dealing with them can be shared there is little chance of anybody seeing themselves as more than a repository for all the nastiness bestowed by society upon the oppressed. There is, of course, much more involved than simply allowing people to have their say. Most women have had their thoughts and opinions systematically devalued since birth; trust and support do not spring up overnight, but need to be carefully nurtured.

The immense value of the small group is a recognition

the women's movement shares with other alternative and radical sections of society. Small groups of people can come together to work on a project for the benefit of its members, or to work with a particular issue, and from experience it seems that a group of between five and fifteen people works best. This number of participants makes it possible for the members to know each other well – the vital prerequisite for the building of trust – and ideally ensures that everybody is heard and included. Most groups – in theory at least – are leaderless; the transition from the traditional committee structure to an apparently amorphous and uncontrollable group has often been a frustrating experience. The casualty rate among such groups is high, yet the very concepts of group success and survival become less important with the realisation that what matters most is that, while the group exists, it does what its members need it to do.

A society, and particularly an economy, that is used to organisation and stability, finds it hard to relate to these experimental forms. The women's movement, together with the green movement and other alternative ways of relating to the world, often receives a bad press for being unorganised, woolly-headed and idealistic. While it is sometimes the case that the reluctance to look at issues of internal power and leadership stems from the fear of unearthing personal and collective skeletons, there are definite advantages to looseness of organisation. Absence of organisation can allow creative flexibility. Woolly-headedness can provide the freedom of vision which leads to inspired lateral thinking. Idealism means having a purpose, knowing exactly why you are doing what you are doing. Words seem to take on a power of their own, especially from critics, but words, as we have seen, are only ways of looking at the world, and practice is much more important than theory.

And it is in practice that the influence of the women's

movement has been the strongest. Why use valuable time writing down theory when there is so much practical work to be done? The upsurge of interest in nurseries, legal centres and refuges, health facilities and peace work, environmental activism and co-operatives, has in large part been the result of the revival of feminism. We are so used to thinking in terms of the thinkers and the doers, the experts and the workers, that even sections of the women's movement have questioned the lack of theory within the movement, often without seeing that the theory is in the doing, the practice is theory in the making. When things are changing very rapidly the integration of theory and practice becomes a positive survival skill; how else can you instantly slot today's new experience into your core of theory? 'Feminism is a call to action,' write Donna Hawxhurst and Sue Morrow in Lisa Tuttle's *Encyclopedia of Feminism*. 'It can never be simply a belief system. Without action, feminism is merely empty rhetoric which cancels itself out.'

Where there are few structures, no leaders, and little dogma, labels begin to lose their importance. Thus the internal labels of the women's movement have gradually become less important over the years, and the earlier rivalries that split the movement are better understood. Radical feminism, socialist feminism, lesbian feminism and revolutionary feminism are fluid and often complementary descriptions and, while the debate can be fruitful and revealing, to be one against another defeats the whole purpose of a liberation movement. Yet there is a danger: one thing does not become another simply by calling it something different, and labels are a very good way of justifying your own actions and writing off the opposition.

Many women in the movement with a partisan political background think of themselves as socialist or communist, and there has been a prolonged love/hate relationship between left-wing politics and feminism. Although radical socialists – many of them women who would identify themselves as feminist – have helped to bring feminist awareness into political life, on many issues the women's movement has developed both theory and practice far beyond contemporary socialism. In particular there is a realisation that the 'eventual revolution' implicit in much left-wing theory does not take account of the 'everyday revolution' that many people involved in practical alternatives are engaged in. Some wait for the revolution, others do it.

Another controversy within the women's movement has concerned the implications of the movement's demand for a self-defined sexuality, and whether heterosexuality can for women ever be a self-defined sexuality. There are many levels on which this can be answered, depending upon one's current definition of sexuality. I shall return to the narrow definition of genital sexuality soon, but first we need to look at the way in which feminism relates to men, and how men relate to feminism.

Questions that women in the movement are currently asking are: Can we live and work with men or not? Is it possible that at least some men can think and act in a non-sexist, non-threatening and understanding way with women, which makes a revolution in men's consciousness conceivable, or are things so hopeless that the only way forward is to create new systems, structures and ways of relating that exclude the active participation of men?

Feminist separatism, which is closely and inevitably tied in with the political and social activism of many lesbian women, is a small but well-defined grouping within the movement, and to some extent these women have answered the question. They believe that there is currently no way in which men can help or work with women and, in examining radical alternatives to hetero-sexual relationships and family structure, separatism provides models for a wide range of ways of relating to people and society.

While often sympathetic to the theory and practice of separatism, most women involved in feminism believe that men have an important part to play in the building of a non-sexist society. As yet, however, the bridges between the women's movement and the male half of human society have hardly started being built. Until strong and well-tested links have been created between women in the women's movement and those men willing to work against sexism, a tolerant and egalitarian society is difficult to envisage. But there is no point in being impatient, and it has been a very necessary process that contemporary feminism has taken a quarter of a century to evolve to its present state. In particular it has been important for women to regain some of their personal power and authority in an environment where patriarchy – the rule of men – was not constantly present.

Many men, and not a few women, have been concerned about the exclusion of men from the meetings and discussions that are part of the process of social change in a society that includes both women and men. It would be easy to simplify the reasons why it is important for any oppressed and socially 'inferior' group of people to exclude the oppressive 'superior' people from their meetings. The main reason is that women need the opportunity to find their individual identity without either being identified with men or feeling that a woman's point of view is being devalued by the thoughts, reflections and expressions of attendant men.

It is also important to recognise that because our society has so differentiated the intimate daily life of men and women, most men have little idea of what women think or feel, and no man has ever experienced the reality of being a woman. Thus a man can never be a feminist in the same way as a woman can. If men were to participate in the process of women identifying and discovering themselves, one of the fundamental purposes of the women's movement would be lost.

How have men responded to the growth of the women's movement? Among the majority of men two attitudes prevail, in many cases being difficult to separate. Laughing it off and laughing at it are very widespread reactions. Laughing it off is a way of not having to look at it at all, laughing at it is a powerful way of maintaining the status quo. Being able to laugh with it is a rare skill, especially when oppression is difficult to see as a laughing matter.

Laughing off the women's movement is one side of a coin of which apparent threat is the reverse. The threat to masculinity from liberated women looms large and works on many levels. There is the practical, everyday level. First these women don't want to do things that women have always done, like wash dishes, floors and nappies; then they take away our freedom by insisting that we be involved in childcare and housecare; then they go out and demand our jobs. Where will it end? Here is Douglas, a fireman interviewed by Anna Ford for her book *Men*: 'I have mixed feelings about women on the team. The brigade is a great all-male preserve. You can be typically male chauvinist. You can make jokes about women, you can swear, you can do what you like. However liberated or friendly a couple of women were who were going to be on the team, you would still be prevented from asserting yourself in the same way.'

Then there is the emotional level. It's hardly surprising that many women who become aware of the limits to their freedom are angry. When you begin to realise, at thirty or forty years old, just how much your life has been controlled and confined, anger is the almost inevitable response. But men in general find women's righteous anger very hard to handle – so it's written off. Anna Ford's interviewees included Hugh, an Essex solicitor: 'Occasionally I come across women's libbers, but I don't like them. I think they're strident, I think they're often humourless, I think they're intolerant, and that's basically what I find unattractive about them.' Tom, a Lancashire miner, puts it down to biology: 'I think people like the Germaine Greers of this world tend to cause trouble and to divide. I have met the emancipated women. I wasn't impressed. I think it's got to be down to the hormone thing.'

For many men who were conscious of the emergence of a range of alternatives in the 1970s and 1980s, the growth of feminism was an interesting problem. The theory was and is totally supportable, but, as the women in their lives found new ways of expressing themselves and began to open themselves to new potential, the new men often felt excluded. They approved of what 'their' women were doing, but felt left out, rejected, even annoyed.

One reaction was to form men's groups modelled on the consciousness-raising groups of the women's movement. Providing a safe environment for men to share their experiences and feelings has helped many men to look at themselves and their relationships in a new light, but has its own challenges.

Men who participate in men's groups often find it very difficult to integrate the hurtful experiences of being male and look at models for the future. There are several linked reasons for this. The first is that most men have had very little practice in examining their personal histories and exploring their feelings about their pasts – as we have seen, being a 'real man' means not acknowledging your feelings, and certainly not admitting that you hurt. The fear of expressing your feelings extends into a fear of sharing important and intimate thoughts and insights with other men, a fear which, judging from the response too often received from other men, is totally justified. All this accumulated fear and hopelessness can easily lead to despair, a sense that the gap between the present situation and a world changed enough to deal with all of our current problems is simply too wide to be bridged. After all, it would mean giving up so much of what is precious in the masculine canon that it seems inconceivable that the world could exist without it. The possible casualties might include sexual performance, heterosexuality, coupledom, power and authority. So much to gain, but so much to lose.

Another feeling common to men gaining an awareness of sexism is guilt. To read the feminist literature, especially books like Susan Brownmiller's *Against Our Will*, Andrea Dworkin's *Pornography: Men Possessing Women*, Heather Formaini's *Men: The Darker Continent* or Rosalind Miles' *The Rites of Man*, is to bring home to men the terrible excesses that men have committed and continue to commit against women. Men are guilty of rampant discrimination, of tragic physical and psychological carnage, and there would appear to be no health in us. The weight of guilt is crushing if you accept it on behalf of all men. It seems that you can either ignore the evidence (and feel guilty about that), or apologise constantly and feel guilty about all the awful things that you and other men have ever done to oppress women.

But guilt is no good, or at least it is no good if it results only in powerlessness, anger and grief. It is mostly no good because the past cannot be changed, only acknowledged and understood. Powerlessness, anger and grief are largely the result of feeling the gap between how things have been and how they might have been, and the only point at which we have any chance of bridging that gap is in the present.

From a woman's point of view, male guilt seems the obvious and deserved counterpart of justified and well-placed blame. Men are to blame for the terrible oppression of patriarchy. Of course they are – nobody else is. But like guilt, blame that cannot be converted to positive action is – while understandable – ultimately pointless. Blaming people for things done in the past is only useful if it helps to understand what happened. All too often it is blaming them for being the only thing they knew how to be in the circumstances. Because blame is usually associated with very negative feelings, if the starting point is blame it is not easy to see the past in the dispassionate way that leads to understanding.

Another thing about blame is to remember the importance of seeing any social structure or grouping as the sum of the individuals within it. Even though it may seem like a drop in the ocean, pointing one man in the direction of one small change for the better rather than blaming him for his failing is well worth the effort. Although blaming men, or the patriarchy, or male-dominated capitalism, for the rampant sexism within our society seems entirely logical, it is an unproductive way of working towards practical change, for it tends to overlook the few avenues currently available through which feminist values are likely to seep into men's consciousnesses.

Close friendships between men, and the support and security that are created when men stop playing games with each other and meet as real human beings, are still too rare in our culture. There is no reason at all why men's friendships with other men cannot be as deep and satisfying as their friendships with women but, because there are few precedents and models, there is a great deal of hard work and soul-searching to be done in this area. It's so easy for the competitive mode of male camaraderie to extend into the arena of personal relationships: I know exactly what it's like to be at the receiving end of 'you're-more-sexist-than-me' propaganda couched as brotherly advice.

If men really want to change things, the acknowledgement and understanding of the past, both personal and social, is critical. The best way to regain the reality of your own past is through sharing it in (sometimes all too sordid) detail with people you trust, and the best way to understand other people's pasts (which collectively make up history) is to listen to them carefully, sensitively and openly.

While men learn to share the details of their personal agendas with one another in safe and supportive ways, one of the main ways in which men are going to discover the potential of a non-sexist society is by creating deep and open relationships with women who have thought deeply about issues of empowerment, choice and communication. The extent to which women are responsible for the liberation of all human beings – both female and male – has long been a subject of feminist debate. It seems clear to me that men cannot and must not rely on women to show them how to sort themselves out; such a course of action only leads to frustration and dependency. On the other hand, women are in a position to show men many of the personal and practical skills needed in a more loving and caring world.

What is needed is a radical and far-reaching programme of skills exchanges, in which we can teach each other the crafts and techniques which have for too long been the domain of half of the human population. Cooking and mending, cleaning and listening, household maintenance and gardening are surely human skills, not exclusively female or male ones.

In our society, women and men much more often meet in single-sex groups than in mixed ones. Men meet at the pub, the club, the match and the races; women at the institute, the corner shop, or when taking the children to school. While there are many groups and organisations offering women and men the opportunity to work and enjoy time together, it is only recently that men and women have started to meet specifically to look in depth at the interactions that go on between them.

I would not for a moment deny the importance of the single-sex group, whether it be a consciousness-raising group, a model railway society or a knitting circle, but I am also convinced that there are important benefits and insights to be gained from men and women meeting together on a regular basis in mixed groups. Whether we feel comfortable in it or not, we all live in a world inhabited by both men and women. Whatever friendships we choose to be our priorities, we are still going to have to work out how we relate to the half of the population who are the other sex from us.

To many people the idea of mixed consciousness-raising groups sounds like a particularly exquisite form of torture, and it's important to remember that the purpose of such a group is to add to the sum of human fulfilment rather than to 'deal with the issues' in a fraught, heavy-handed, confrontative way. On the other hand, the exploration of important and sometimes painful issues won't always be sweetness and light.

As in all relating, working on big issues in mixed groups will often hit the rocks of blame and guilt, duty and frustration, and we can easily come to imagine that the reason why things are not as they should be is entirely due to the presence of a person or people of the other sex. Sometimes this will be true, but that doesn't necessarily make them the enemy, to be written off from here on in.

When things get too difficult we can always choose to withdraw to the comparative safety of people who, being the same sex as us, feel easier to be with. But ultimately this won't make the problems go away. Though it might ease things in the short term, it won't make any radical difference to the society we live in. Eventually the problems, the frustrations and the difficulties need to be faced and, since many of those difficulties are to do with relating to one or more people of the other sex, the importance of the mixed group in providing the immediate stimulus for helping to deal with these difficulties is crucial.

Women's anger towards men is a good case in point. As we have seen, it is virtually inevitable that many women in our society will be angry, quite justifiably angry, about their treatment at the hands of men. Many women find it hard in an all-woman group, or with a female therapist, to express that anger, because they find it hard to shout 'at' another woman. After all, it's men they feel angry towards, and shouting at another woman simply doesn't feel right. To have an actual man there to shout at is usually far more satisfying, and at the same time it can help the man to be able to listen to and hear that woman's anger without running away from it.

Where does all this leave sex and physical intimacy? My sense is that while we are consciously working towards an alternative model of intimate relating, we may well have to forgo, for a while at least, many of our expectations about shared physical sexuality. Where intimacy has become so laden with fear and threat, it may be necessary to take the closest forms of intimacy much more slowly. And as I said earlier, sexual performance may well be a casualty of our new-found friendship. To take intimacy slowly is not to underrate the pleasure and fun of sexuality, it is simply to acknowledge the years of patterning that have made non-possessive and non-threatening sex a very rare phenomenon.

Old patterns die hard. It is terribly easy to look at what is wrong with the world and be overwhelmed. But powerlessness changes nothing. It only allows those who wield power over others to continue in their oppression, and encourages those who believe that oppression is divinely ordained and wonderfully natural. Until we see each and every person in the world as a prime candidate for liberation into personal power, equal to us but excitingly different from us, we shall stay locked into our expectations and limitations. The whole point about being human is that we can choose our future; history and experience are illuminating but not limiting.

Yet it is tempting to fall into the opposite trap of being so positive that we ignore the reality of the world we live in. Positivity is the wonderfully uplifting experience of realising that we are not limited, but it is also the hope that is so often dashed on the rocks of everyday experience. The world we have created is not always friendly and welcoming, yet the harsh realities of ugliness and depression often blind us to the joy and inspiration which, if we can recognise them, provide more than reason enough for sustained optimism. We have to live in the world, *and* we have to know that we have the power to change it through our own example. To do this we first have to empower ourselves, to believe in ourselves.

The future, as we are so often told, is in our hands. The reason we have been told it so often is that other people have believed that their vision will do for us too, and they have assumed that 'our hands' are yours and mine linked with those who think they know what is best for us. But the truth is that only you and I know what is best for us, and only you and I know our full potential and the things that prevent us from achieving it.

Bibliography

Arcana, Judith, *Every Mother's Son*, The Women's Press, 1983

Ardrey, Robert, *The Territorial Imperative*, Fontana, 1967

Baker, Carolyn and Freebody, Peter, *Children's First School Books*, Basil Blackwell, 1989

Barbach, Lonnie, *For Yourself*, Doubleday, 1975

Barrett, Michèle and McIntosh, Mary, *The Anti-Social Family*, Verso, 1982

Belotti, Elena, *Little Girls*, Writers and Readers, 1975

Berger, John, *Ways of Seeing*, Penguin, 1972

Bernard, Jessie, *The Future of Marriage*, Penguin, 1976

Brownmiller, Susan, *Against Our Will*, Penguin, 1976

Butler, Sandra, *Conspiracy of Silence*, New Glide, 1978

Carter, Angela, *The Sadean Woman*, Virago, 1977

Cartledge, Sue and Joanna Ryan (ed.), *Sex and Love*, The Women's Press, 1983

Comer, Lee, *Wedlocked Women*, Feminist Books, 1974

Comfort, Alex, *The Joy of Sex*, Quartet, 1972

Cook, Mark and McHenry, Robert, *Sexual Attraction*, Pergamon, 1978

Dickson, Anne, *A Woman in Her Own Right*, Quartet, 1982

Douglas, Nik and Slinger, Penny, *Sexual Secrets*, Destiny Books, 1979

Dowling, Collette, *The Cinderella Complex*, Fontana, 1982

Dworkin, Andrea, *Pornography: Men Possessing Women*, The Women's Press, 1981

Dworkin, Andrea, *Our Blood*, The Women's Press, 1982

Firestone, Shulamith, *The Dialectic of Sex*, Bantam, 1971

Fisher, Elizabeth, *Woman's Creation: Sexual Evolution and the Shaping of Society*, McGraw-Hill, 1980

Ford, Anna, *Men*, Corgi, 1985

Formaini, Heather, *Men: The Darker Continent*, Mandarin, 1991

Frankham, Jo, and Stronach, Ian, *Making a Drama out of a Crisis*, Centre for Applied Research in Education, University of East Anglia, 1990

Friedan, Betty, *The Feminine Mystique*, Norton, 1963

Greer, Germaine, *The Female Eunuch*, MacGibbon and Kee, 1970

Haddon, Celia, and Prentice, Thomson, *Stronger Love, Safer Sex*, Macmillan, 1989

Hayman, Susie, *Say Yes, Say No, Say Maybe?*, Brook Advisory Centres, 1991

Hite, Shere, *The Hite Report on Male Sexuality*, Macdonald, 1981

Hite, Shere, *Women and Love*, Viking, 1988

Hooper, Anne, *The Body Electric*, Virago, 1980

Jackson, Stevi, *Childhood and Sexuality*, Basil Blackwell, 1983

Jennings, Paula, letter to WIRES, reprinted in *Love Your Enemy? The Debate Between Heterosexual Feminism and Political Lesbianism*, Onlywomen Press, 1981

Kahn, Sandra, *The Ex-Wife Syndrome*, Ebury, 1990

Kitzinger, Sheila, *Women's Experience of Sex*, Penguin, 1985

Lakoff, Robin, *Language and Woman's Place*, Harper and Row, 1975

Lawson, Annette, *Adultery*, Basil Blackwell, 1989

Lazarre, Jane, *On Loving Men*, Virago, 1981

Lloyd, Barbara, and Archer, John (ed.), Exploring Sex Differences, Academic Press, 1976

Lorenz, Konrad, *On Aggression*, Methuen, 1966

Lowndes Sevely, Josephine, *Eve's Secrets*, Bloomsbury, 1987

McBride, Will, *Show Me*, Harper and Row, 1980

Meulenbelt, Anja, *The Shame is Over*, The Women's Press, 1980

Meulenbelt, Anja, *For Ourselves*, Sheba, 1981

Miles, Rosalind, *The Rites of Man*, Grafton, 1991

Miller, Casey, and Swift, Kate, *A Handbook of Non-Sexist Writing*, The Women's Press, 1981

Miller, Jill, *Happy as a Dead Cat*, The Women's Press, 1980

Millett, Kate, *Sexual Politics*, Virago, 1977

Morin, Jack, *Men Loving Themselves*, Down There Press, 1980

Mosley, Fran, *Everyone Counts*, ILEA, 1985

Newsom, John and Elizabeth, Diane Richardson and Joyce Scaife, 'Perspectives in Sex-Role Stereotyping', in Chetwynd, Jane, and Hartnett, Oonagh (ed.), *The Sex Role System*, Routledge and Kegan Paul, 1978

O'Neill, Nena and George, *Open Marriage*, Abacus, 1975

Peckham, Morse, *Art and Pornography*, Harper and Row, 1971

Piercy, Marge, *Woman on the Edge of Time*, The Women's Press, 1979

Priestland, Gerald, *The Future of Violence*, Hamish Hamilton, 1974

Proto, Louis, *The Feeling Good Book*, Thorsons, 1982

Raimy, Eric, *Shared Houses, Shared Lives*, Tarcher, 1979

Read, Sue, *Sexual Harassment at Work*, Penguin, 1983

Russ, Joanna, *Magic Mommas, Trembling Sisters, Puritans and Perverts*, Crossing Press, 1985

Schultz, Terri, *Bittersweet*, Penguin, 1979

Sebastyen, Amanda, 'Assumptions in the Women's Movement', in Friedman, Scarlet, and Sarah, Elizabeth (ed.), *On The Problem of Men*, The Women's Press, 1982

Segal, Lynn, *Slow Motion*, Virago, 1990

Shiers, John, 'One Step to Heaven', in Cant, Bob, and Hemmings, Susan (ed.) *Radical Records: Thirty Years of Lesbian and Gay History*, Routledge, 1988

Smithers, Alan, and Zientek, Pauline, *Gender, Primary Schools and the National Curriculum*, NASUWT, 1991

Sonkin, Daniel, and Durphy, Michael, *Learning to Live Without Violence*, Volcano, 1982

Spender, Dale, *Man-Made Language*, Routledge, 1980

Spender, Dale, *There's Always Been a Women's Movement This Century*, Pandora, 1983

Stassinopoulos, Arianna, *The Female Woman*, Davis-Poynter, 1973

Tripp, C.A., *The Homosexual Matrix*, McGraw Hill, 1978

Tuttle, Lisa, *Encyclopedia of Feminism*, Arrow, 1987

Tweedie, Jill, *It's Only Me*, Methuen, 1983

Ullian, Dorothy, 'The Development of Conceptions of Masculinity and Femininity', in Lloyd, Barbara, and Archer, John (ed.), *Exploring Sex Differences*, Academic Press, 1976

Visual Dictionary of Sex, Pan, 1979

Wallsgrove, Ruth, 'Pornography: Between the Devil and the True Blue Whitehouse', *Spare Rib Reader*, Penguin, 1982

Weideger, Paula, *Female Cycles*, The Women's Press, 1978

Wex, Marianne, *Let's Take Back Our Space*, Hermine Fees, 1979

Young, Wayland, *Eros Denied*, Weidenfeld and Nicolson, 1965

Zilbergeld, Bernie, *Male Sexuality*, Fontana, 1975

If you would like to know more about Optima books, a catalogue is available from Little, Brown, 165 Great Dover St, London SE1 4YA.

All Optima books are available at your bookshop or newsagent, or can be ordered from the following address:
Optima Books
Cash Sales Department
PO Box 11
Falmouth
Cornwall TR10 9EN.

Alternatively you may fax your order to the above address. Fax number 0326 76423.

Payments can be made as follows: cheque, postal order (payable to Little, Brown & Co (Publishers) Ltd) or by credit cards, Visa/Access. *Do not send cash or currency*.

UK customers, please send a cheque or postal order (no currency) and allow 80p for postage and packing for the first book plus 20p for each additional book up to a maximum charge of £2.00.

BFPO customers, please allow 80p for the first book plus 20p for each additional book.

Overseas customers, including Ireland, please allow £1.50 for postage and packing for the first book, £1.00 for the second book and 30p for each additional book.

NAME (Block Letters) ....

ADDRESS ....

....

☐ I enclose my remittance for   _____

☐ I wish to pay by Access/Visa Card

Number ☐☐☐☐☐☐☐☐☐☐☐☐☐☐☐☐

Card Expiry Date ☐☐☐☐